The Metropolitan Museum of Art
Favorite Paintings

The Metropolitan

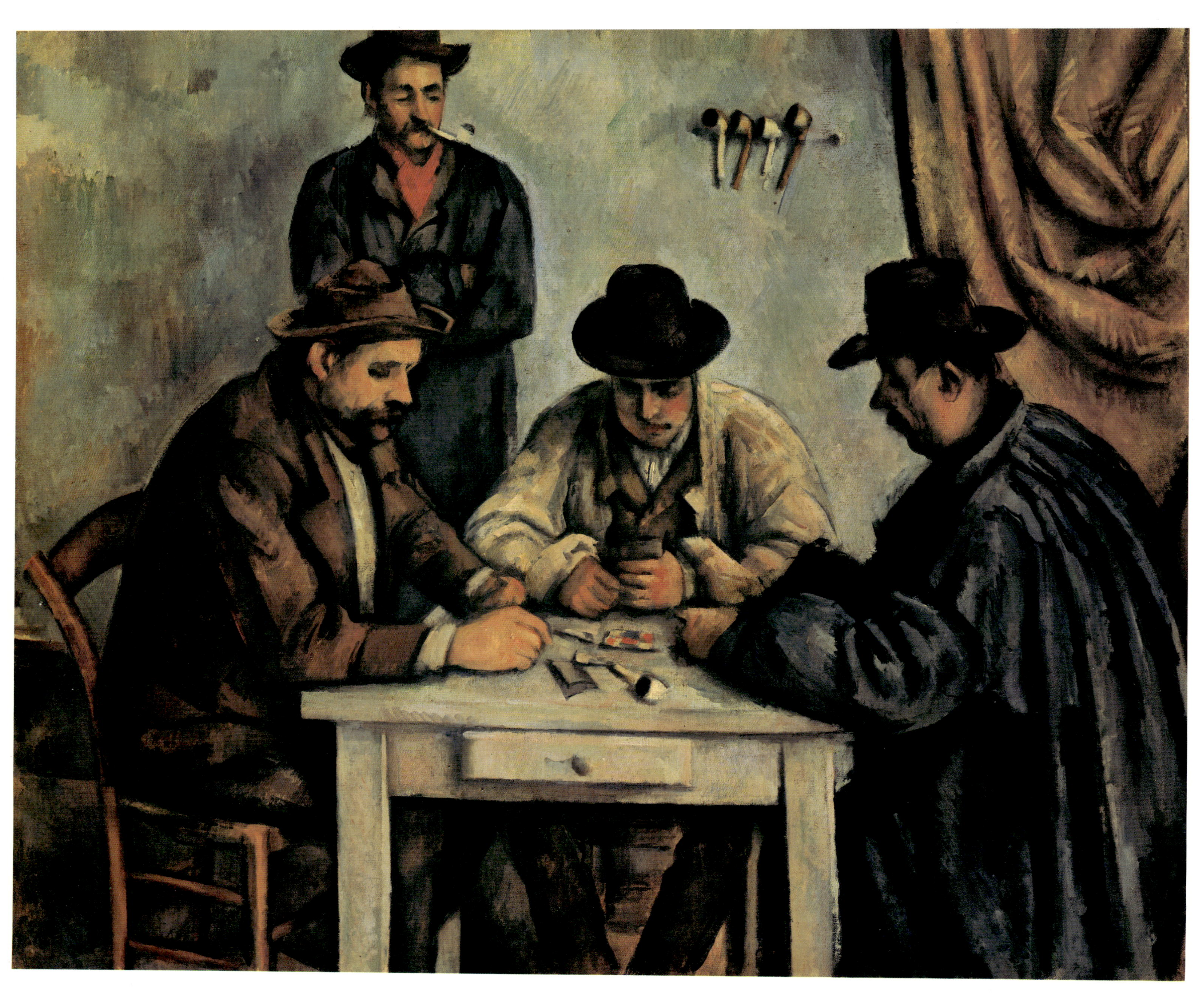

Museum of Art

Favorite Paintings

INTRODUCTION AND COMMENTARIES BY

A. HYATT MAYOR

Curator Emeritus of Prints
The Metropolitan Museum of Art

AN Artabras BOOK

CROWN PUBLISHERS, INC. • NEW YORK, N.Y.

FRONT COVER
Portrait of a Young Woman (detail) by Piero del Pollaiuolo

TITLE PAGE
The Card Players by Paul Cézanne

BACK COVER
Study for *A Sunday Afternoon at La Grande Jatte*
by Georges-Pierre Seurat

Commentaries on page 112

Library of Congress Cataloging in Publication Data

New York (City). Metropolitan Museum of Art.
Favorite paintings from the Metropolitan Museum of Art.

1. Painting—New York (City)—Catalogs. 2. New York (City). Metropolitan Museum of Art—Catalogs. I. Mayor, Alpheus Hyatt, 1901— II. Title.
N610.A527 750'.74'01471 78-11404
ISBN 0-517-53551-3

CONTENTS

Commentary on page 112

INTRODUCTION

If you were asked to pick fifty-four paintings—and no more—out of the thousands in The Metropolitan Museum, which would you choose? Many of your choices would, I hope, appear in this book, but many certainly would not, because no two people ever prefer exactly the same things. I have selected paintings that quicken my pulse, that have some historical importance, and that line up in a kind of skeleton map of the Museum's extensive collection. In general, the Metropolitan is strong in the Northern, and especially the Dutch, schools because New York's interest was aroused in 1909 by the Hudson–Fulton Exhibition that commemorated Henry Hudson's exploration of the river in 1609 and Robert Fulton's start of steam navigation there in 1809. The Hudson–Fulton show dominated local taste for decades by presenting the first large showing of early American furniture and by gathering some three dozen Rembrandt paintings, as well as works by Hals and others, in the first great Dutch painting show ever held outside Europe. The Metropolitan owes its other very great specialty—French Impressionist paintings—to Mrs. H. O. Havemeyer's bequest in 1929 of the matchless collection that she formed with the help of Mary Cassatt. This great gift brought more fine donations from Sam A. Lewisohn, Stephen C. Clark, Robert Lehman, and others.

But these glories are here only because of the determination of many brave and hopeful workers. In 1870, a few months after the Museum had been chartered, but still had nothing to show, one of the founding trustees, William T. Blodgett, secured a group of 174 old paintings in Paris, for which he and our first president, John Taylor Johnston, advanced the money in the hope of being repaid by public subscription. They were repaid and deserved the confidence, for they were luckier than many Americans who plunged for art in those days, since their haul included a fine Poussin and an exquisite Guardi of the Rialto. Then for seventeen years few paintings came until Catharine Lorillard Wolfe bequeathed her collection of 143 contemporary paintings, many being landscapes of the Barbizon School, along with a fund whose income was used to purchase Homer's *Gulf Stream,* Goya's *Bullfight,* Daumier's *Don Quixote,* Renoir's *Madame Charpentier and her Children* (page 77), and many more outstanding paintings.

In 1889 the galleries were transformed by two gifts. Erwin Davis gave the first two Manets that ever entered a public collection—the *Woman with a Parrot* (page 69) and the *Boy with a Sword*—which he had bought on the advice of the painter Julian Alden Weir. And our second president, Henry Gurdon Marquand, gave thirty-seven paintings that he had selected with a discernment that astonishes in a busy banker at a time when there were no handy monographs, no photographic archives to guide one. His gift included such masterpieces as the Vermeer *Young Woman with a Water Jug* (page 47); van Dyck's *Duke of Richmond and Lennox* (page 39); three Hals portraits; and paintings by Petrus Christus, Ruisdael, Gainsborough, and many more that have steadily been on exhibition.

The systematic composition of the collection began in 1904 when J. Pierpont Morgan became president, until his death nine years later, and the bequest of Jacob Rogers at last endowed the Museum with sufficient funds to compete in the world market. Morgan at once secured the most acute connoisseur of the age, Roger Fry in London, to act as purchasing agent for five stormy years until the two determined wills clashed and, alas, parted. But Fry left in his place a young painter, Bryson Burroughs, who shared his range of perception. Their remarkable purchases included Veronese's *Mars and Venus* (page 27), Carpaccio's *Meditation on the Passion,* Giotto's *Epiphany,* Botticelli's *Three Miracles of Saint Zenobius,* and the first Renoir ever bought by a public museum—the portrait of *Madame Char-*

pentier and her Children (page 77). In 1913 Burroughs bought Cézanne's *Colline des Pauvres* out of the Armory Show; it was the first Cézanne ever purchased by an American museum.

The collecting of American paintings began in earnest when George A. Hearn in 1906 and 1911 gave a fund for the purchase of paintings by living American artists. The Hearn Funds and the Morris K. Jessup Fund given in 1915 have been used to build up a unique series of American paintings, whose comprehensive range will become apparent when room for showing a sizeable selection of them will be provided for the first time by the opening of the expanded American Wing.

The growing activity of the Museum began to attract the gift of great collections. In 1913 Benjamin Altman's splendid bequest of his wide-ranging collection included Botticelli's late *Last Communion of Saint Jerome,* the *Portrait of a Man* by Giorgione or Titian, Hals' *Merrymakers at Shrovetide* (page 41) and paintings by Memling and Velázquez. In 1916 the young J. P. Morgan gave the only Raphael altarpiece outside Europe (page 23), to which the Museum added one of the five predella panels in 1932. In 1929 the painting galleries were once again transformed by Mrs. Havemeyer's bequest of her celebrated collection, which brought in Bronzino's *Portrait of a Young Man* (page 29); El Greco's *Cardinal Guevara* and his *View of Toledo* (page 33); Goya's *Majas on a Balcony* (page 61); and her famous series of French paintings by Courbet, Daumier (page 67), Degas (pages 79 and 81), Manet, Monet (page 89), Renoir, and Cézanne. The exhibition of the Havemeyer collection as a whole brought cheer to the Depression, while its wise dispersal throughout the museum spreads her name and her taste into the widest possible view.

During the lean 1930s the Museum managed to buy van Eyck's *Crucifixion and Last Judgment* (page 13), Watteau's *Mezzetin* (page 49), and Titian's late *Venus and the Lute Player* (page 25), while Harry Payne Bingham gave Rubens's beautiful *Venus and Adonis,* and the Michael Friedsam Collection brought great early Northern paintings, including the mysterious *Annunciation* attributed to Jan van Eyck (page 15).

In the 1940s Maitland F. Griggs bequeathed Sassetta's fantastical *Journey of the Magi* (page 19) with other fine early Italian panels, and the Jules Bache Collection gave the public Titian's *Venus and Adonis,* Crivelli's exquisitely preserved *Madonna,* Rembrandt's *Standard Bearer,* and Goya's red-trousered *Manuel Osorio* with his magpie and cats. In 1950 the bequest of Edward S. Harkness featured Pollaiuolo's profile *Portrait of a Young Lady* (front cover) and Lawrence's *Elizabeth Farren* (page 57). A year later Sam A. Lewisohn left Seurat's finished study for *La Grande Jatte* (back cover), Gauguin's *Ia Orana Maria* (page 85), and van Gogh's *L'Arlésienne* (page 91). In 1960 Stephen C. Clark bequeathed Cézanne's *Card Players* (frontispiece) with other fine French paintings.

Very important purchases were also made, such as El Greco's *Vision of Saint John,* Georges de La Tour's *Fortune Teller,* Chardin's *Boy Blowing Bubbles* (page 53), Tiepolo's three huge battle scenes painted for Ca' Dolfin in Venice, Velázquez's *Juan de Pareja* (page 35), and Rembrandt's *Aristotle with a Bust of Homer* (page 43)—which is the Metropolitan's only great Rembrandt that was not the gift of some generous New Yorker.

The very latest gifts have been among the greatest. In 1975 the Robert Lehman Collection brought the last gathering in American private hands that truly represents Western art since 1300. The splendid paintings are too numerous even to start listing them. We reproduce Botticelli's intensely personal *Annunciation* (page 17). Mr. and Mrs. Charles Wrightsman have managed, in these picked-over times, to find and give such wonderful paintings as Tiepolo's finished sketch for the ceiling in the Würzburg Residenz, David's *Portrait of Monsieur and Madame Lavoisier* (page 55), and de La Tour's haunting *Magdalen*.

It has taken over a century of gifts of paintings and of funds for purchasing to build up a gallery remarkable for its comprehensiveness and its quality. The achievement of so many devoted people can only be hinted at through the selection reproduced in the following pages.

A. Hyatt Mayor

The Metropolitan Museum of Art
Favorite Paintings

Robert Campin, active by 1406, died 1444, *Flemish*

THE ANNUNCIATION Center panel from the Mérode Altarpiece (c. 1425)

HERE FOR THE FIRST TIME the Angel does not greet Mary against a blank background, or among formal columns, or outdoors, but in a cozily furnished, ordinary home. Religious subjects had begun to be domesticated a few years before in humble woodcuts, but this is the first formal altar painting that shows a sacred scene in a familiar, everyday room. The innovation must have caused a sensation, for the central panel was often copied or adapted. Though every object might have been bought at a local shop, each one symbolizes something. The Virgin's purity is shown by the clean towel, the fresh water in the hanging basin, and the white lily. She acts out her humility by sitting on the floor beside a bench that she might have used for a throne. The light of God's emanation divides into seven rays for the seven gifts of the Holy Spirit; it passes through the window without shattering the glass, the way Mary can conceive without losing her virginity. The smoking candle probably refers to Proverbs 24:20, "The candle of the wicked shall be put out."

This pioneer painting of Northern art has a remarkable history: For over five hundred years it belonged to the Belgian family that had commissioned it, until it was bought by the Museum for The Cloisters.

Oil on wood
Center panel 25 3/16 × 24 7/8"
Left wing 25 3/8 × 10 3/4"
Right wing 25 3/8 × 10 5/16"
Purchase, The Cloisters Collection

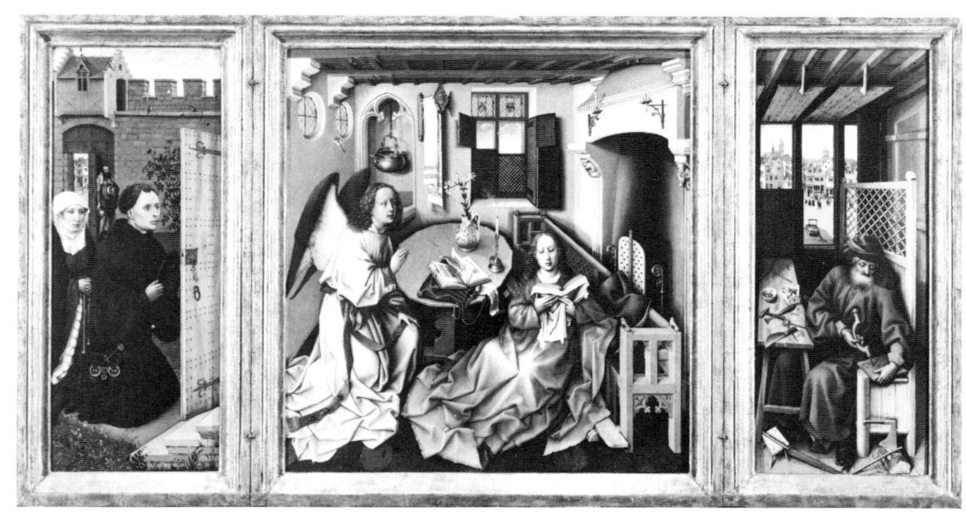

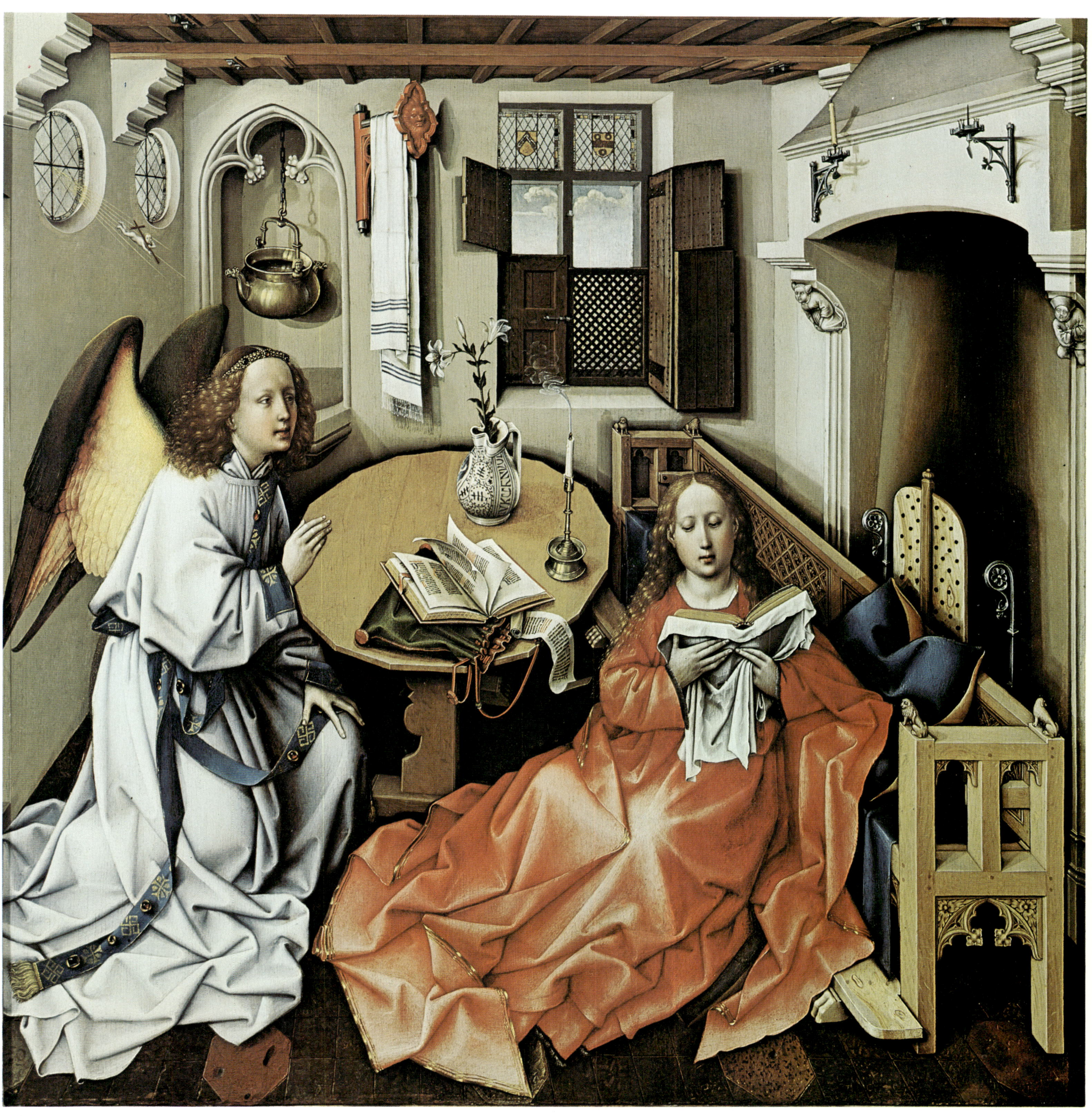

Jan van Eyck, active by 1422, died 1441, *Flemish*

THE CRUCIFIXION AND THE LAST JUDGMENT (c. 1425)

THESE PANELS MAY ONCE have been hinged to a wide central painting that has disappeared. Yet these two subjects make a unit in themselves by pairing Christ's sacrifice on the Cross with His return to judge the results. The original frames (seldom preserved) bear inscriptions that clarify the subjects, which are not divided into right and left, as usual, but up and down. In the *Last Judgment* at the right, Death's bat wings shut out the light of salvation from Hell below, just where the lettering says *VMBRA MORTIS* (the shadow of Death). Christ on the Cross is stripped absolutely naked as a degradation from which even the thieves are spared. He is the shorn lamb of the frame quotation from Acts 8:32: "Like a lamb dumb before his shearer, so opened he not his mouth." Van Eyck made theological abstractions tragically, terribly real with a technique of oil painting that he perfected and all Europe adopted.

Tempera and oil on canvas, transferred from wood
Each 22¼ × 7¾″
Fletcher Fund, 1932

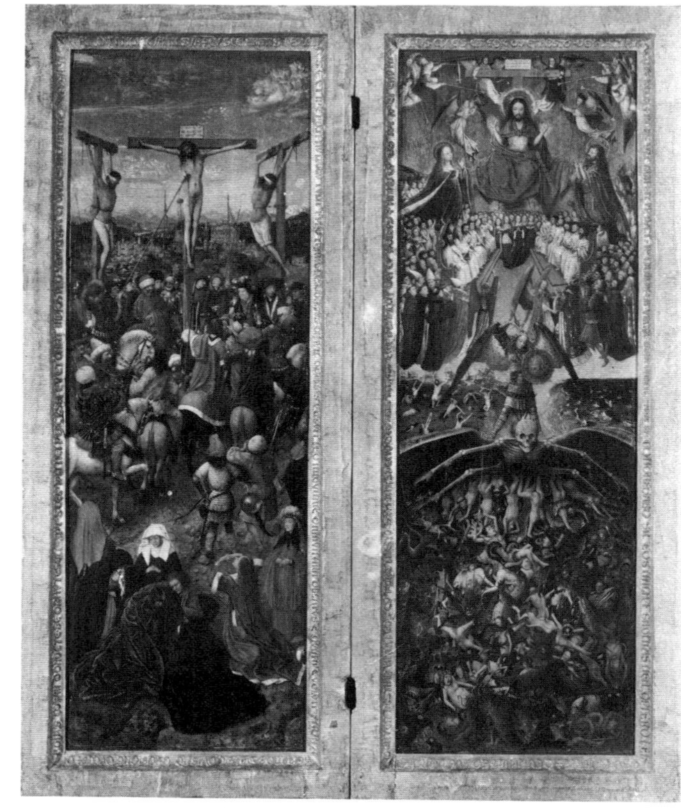

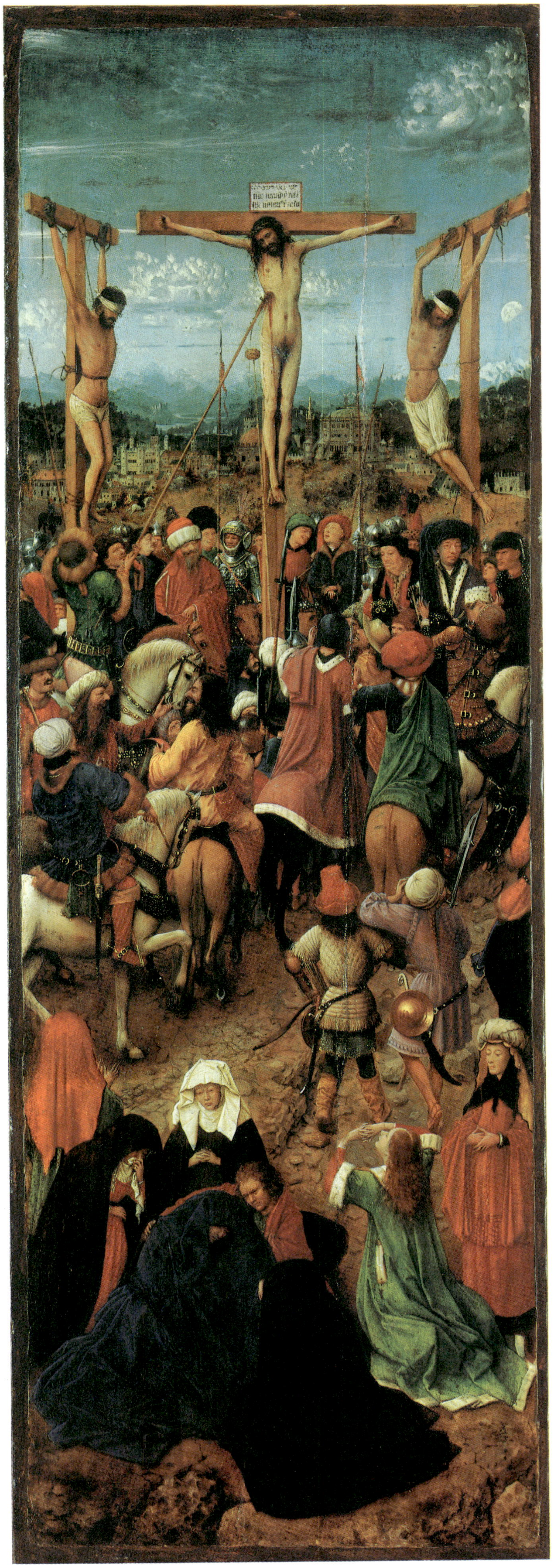

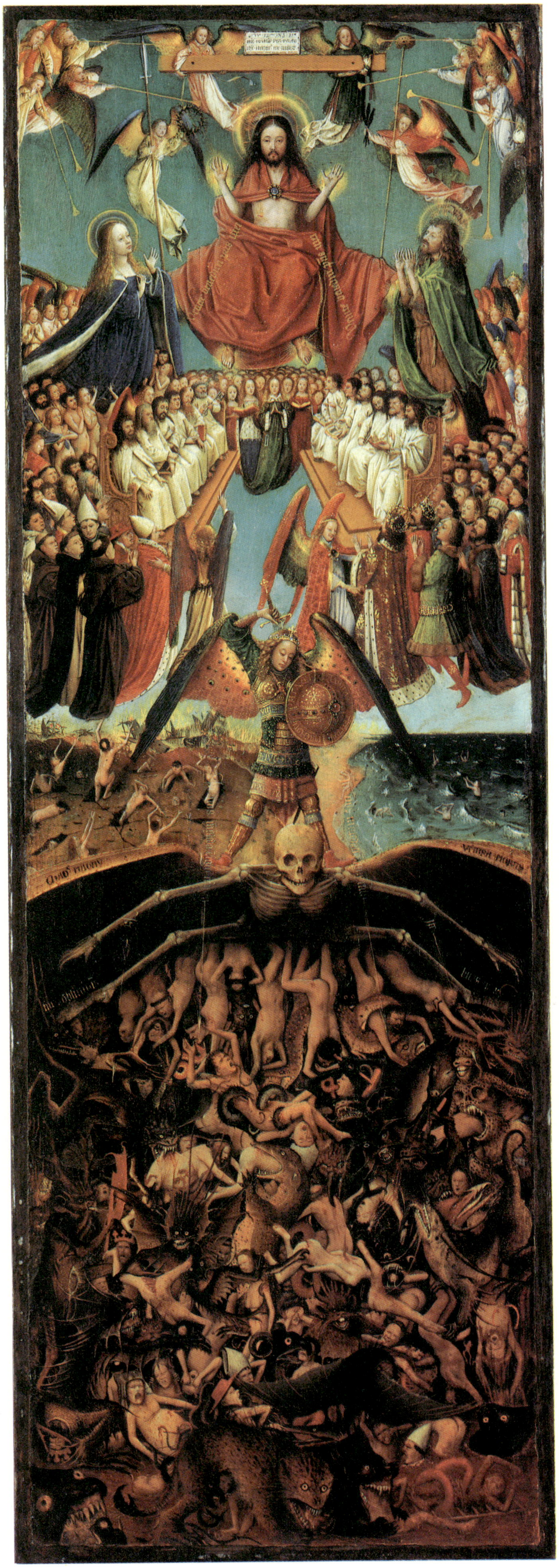

Jan van Eyck (ATTRIBUTED TO) active by 1422, died 1441, *Flemish*

THE ANNUNCIATION

THIS IS THE MOST ERUDITE and symbolic of the three Annunciations illustrated in this volume. We look strangely down on the church front that turns away from us. Every detail has meaning. At Mary's right the new faith of revelation is symbolized by the window that admits God's illumination into the church, and by the flower—called in Flemish a "cross flower"—carved above the buttress in the contemporary Gothic style. On her left, the Old Testament is symbolized by the old Romanesque buttress bearing the two pillars of the porch of Solomon's Temple over a monkey, the animal of evil. The titles at Mary's feet spell *REGINA CELI LET(ARE)* – "Queen of Heaven rejoice"—from the Virgin's Easter antiphon. Before the threshold lies a kicked and battered stone, because Saint Paul wrote to the Romans, "Behold, I lay in Sion a stumbling stone and rock of offence, and whosoever believeth in Him shall not be ashamed." Crooked, untended paths converge on the sanctuary through flowers choked under weeds and past a wall falling into ruin. The enclosed garden of Mary's purity needs Christ as a gardener, the way he appeared to Mary Magdalen after the Crucifixion. When the Messiah eventually comes, his image will fill the empty niche over the door.

Tempera and oil on wood 30½ × 25⅜"
Bequest of Michael Friedsam, 1931
The Friedsam Collection

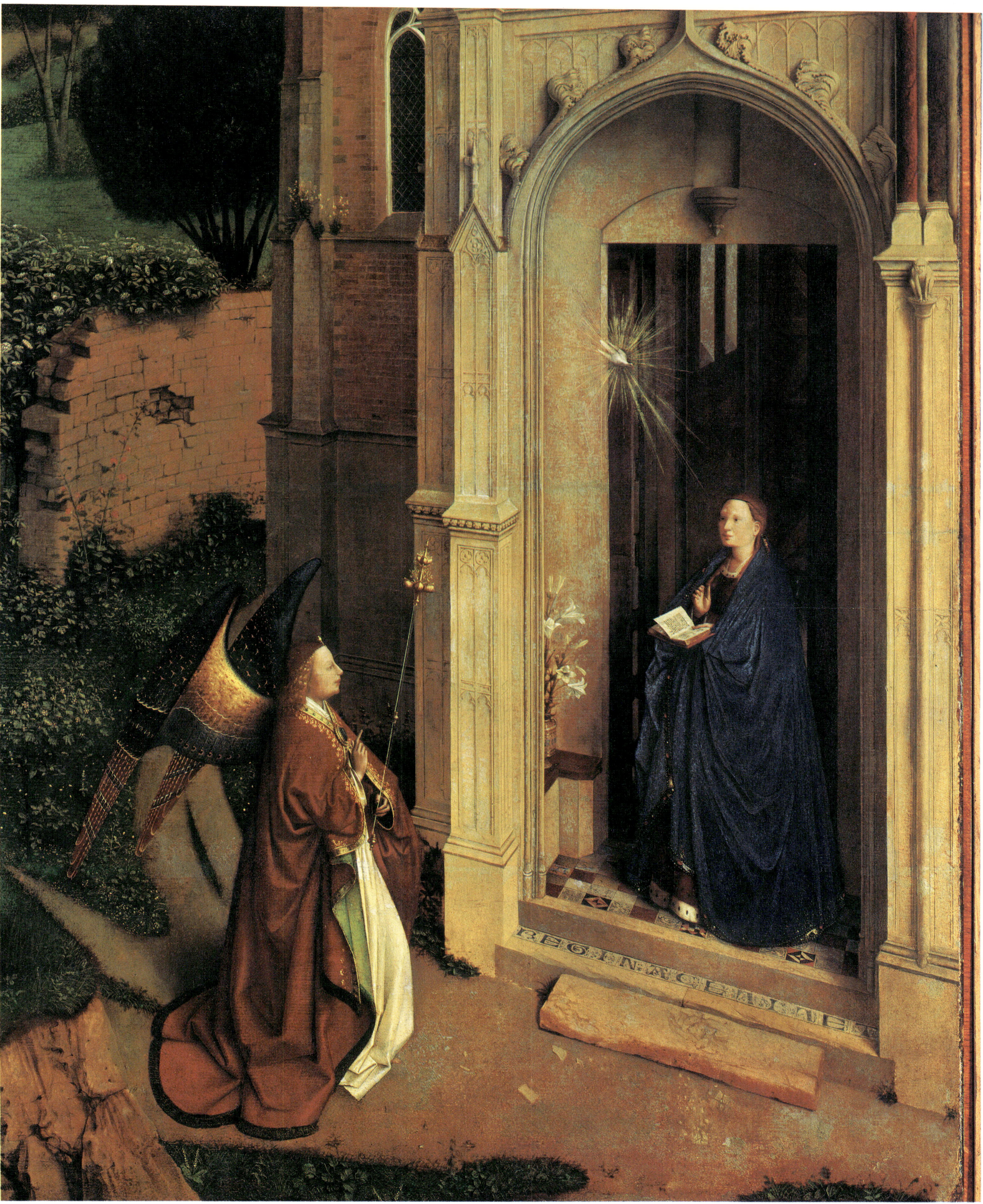

Sandro Botticelli (ALESSANDRO DI MARIANO DEI FILIPEPI), 1444/45–1510, *Italian*

THE ANNUNCIATION

THIS LITTLE PANEL MUST have been commissioned for private prayers, not for a church. Botticelli painted it late in life, after he had renounced the lyric voluptuousness of the *Primavera* and the *Birth of Venus* under the lash of Savonarola's puritanism. Religious conversion concentrated the drive of his energy but did not lead him to the intricate symbolism of the *Annunciation* attributed to Jan van Eyck (page 15). Botticelli's refinements are not theological but visual. He shifts the pair of figures to right of center so as to clear a space where the angel can enter, out of astral distances, for his implosion into the Virgin's retirement. The vehemence of these figures has to be held in check by the strict grid of walls and floor. A sense of architecture organizes all Italian art.

Tempera on panel
9⅜ × 14⅜″
Robert Lehman Collection, 1975

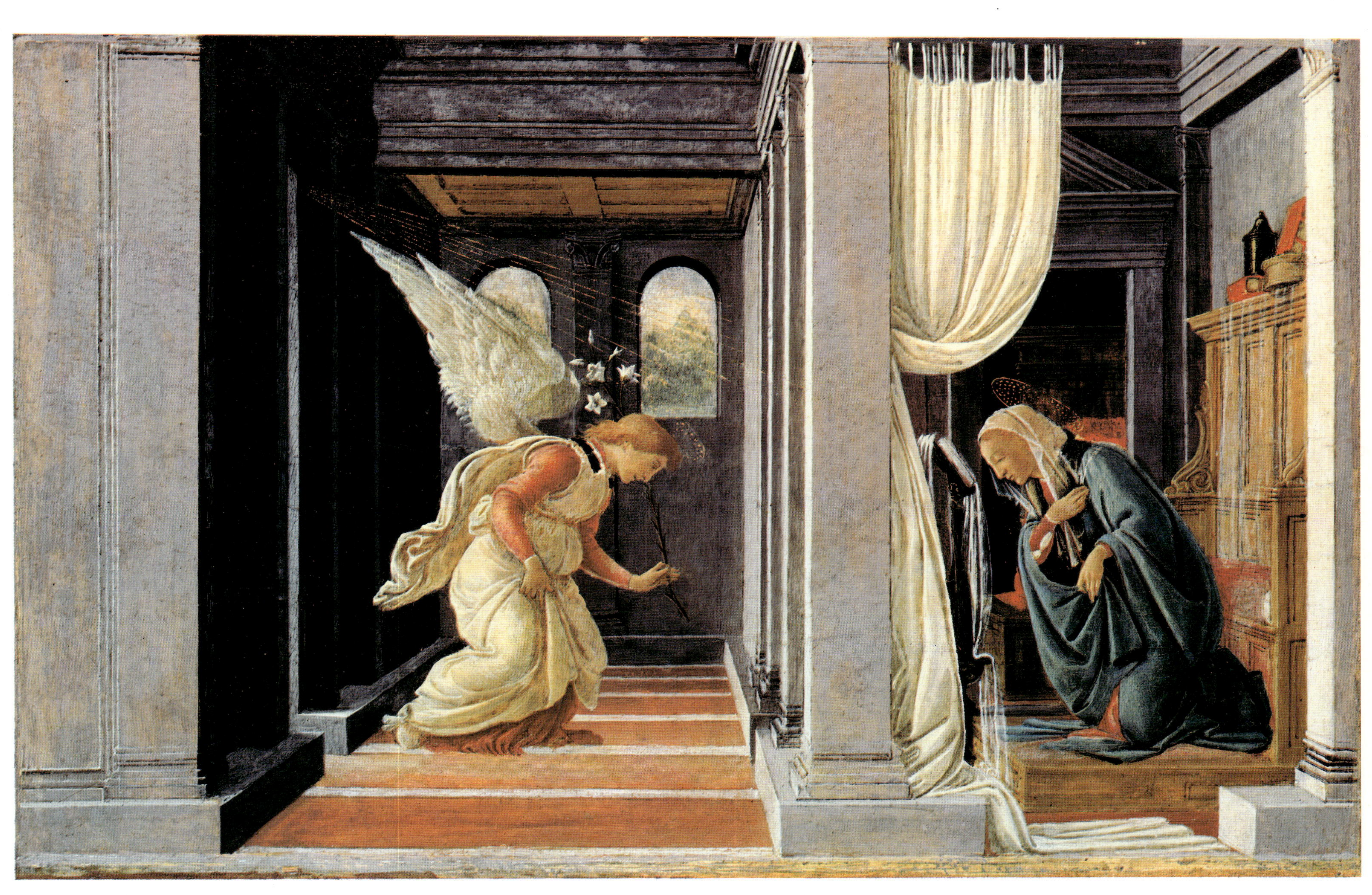

Sassetta (STEFANO DI GIOVANNI), 1392–1450/1451, *Italian*

THE JOURNEY OF THE MAGI (c. 1435)

ALTHOUGH THIS PICTURE LOOKS COMPLETE, it is only the upper half of a tall panel that was sawed in two long ago. The gold star on the hillside points down to the missing manger where the Magi deliver their gifts to the Christ Child; that portion is now in a private collection in Siena. With such a motley procession to organize, it is no wonder that the Magi took twelve days to reach their destination. They bring symbolic gifts to little Jesus—gold for him as King, incense as God, myrrh as Man—and, surely, the monkey lolling at royal ease on muleback must be to amuse him in his natural state of Infant. Sassetta was typically Sienese in turning a sacred subject into a fairy tale of a kind that does not occur in the rational intensity of Florence. Dante expressed a puritanical Florentine disapproval when he called his neighbors *i vani Sanesi,* the silly Sienese. This happy innocence is their charm for us today.

Tempera on wood 8½ × 11¾″
Bequest of Maitland F. Griggs, 1943
Maitland F. Griggs Collection

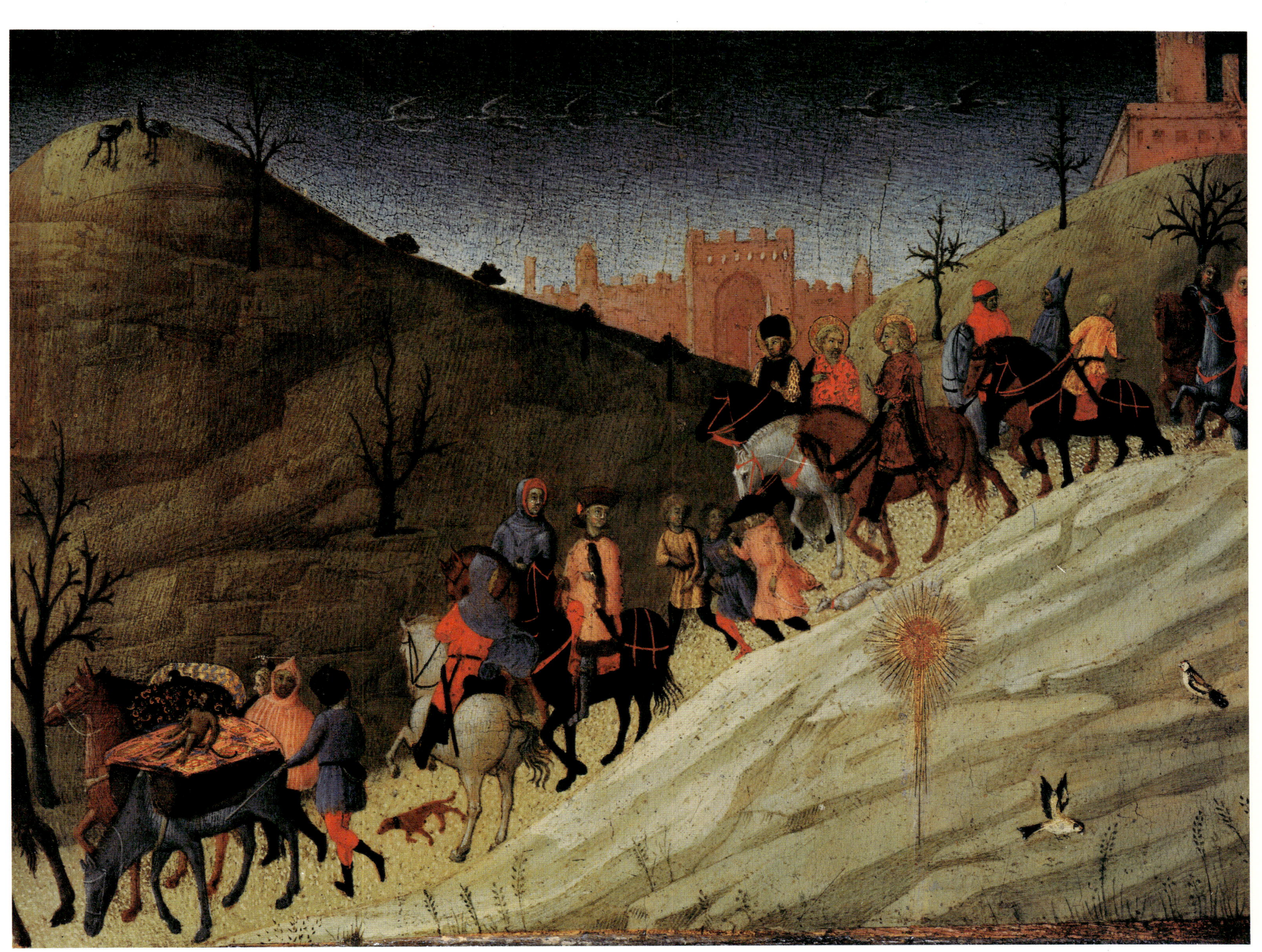

Andrea Mantegna, c. 1430–1506, *Italian*

THE ADORATION OF THE SHEPHERDS (c. 1450–55)

THE VIRGIN'S CELESTIAL translucence makes a sharp contrast with the shepherds' rags, famished faces, and distorted stooping. Such drudges resulted when conquerors could not quite enslave a population, but could impose restrictions that chained the serfs to their fields. In the late 1600s La Bruyère turned his courtier's eye on such people who were more deformed than any class is today: "Here and there in the country one sees certain wild animals, male and female, discolored, sun-scorched, clutching at the earth that they doggedly stir and dig. They produce something like an articulate voice, and when they straighten up on their hind legs, they show a human face, for, in fact, they are men."

Tempera on canvas, transferred from wood 15¾ × 21⅞"
Anonymous Gift, 1932

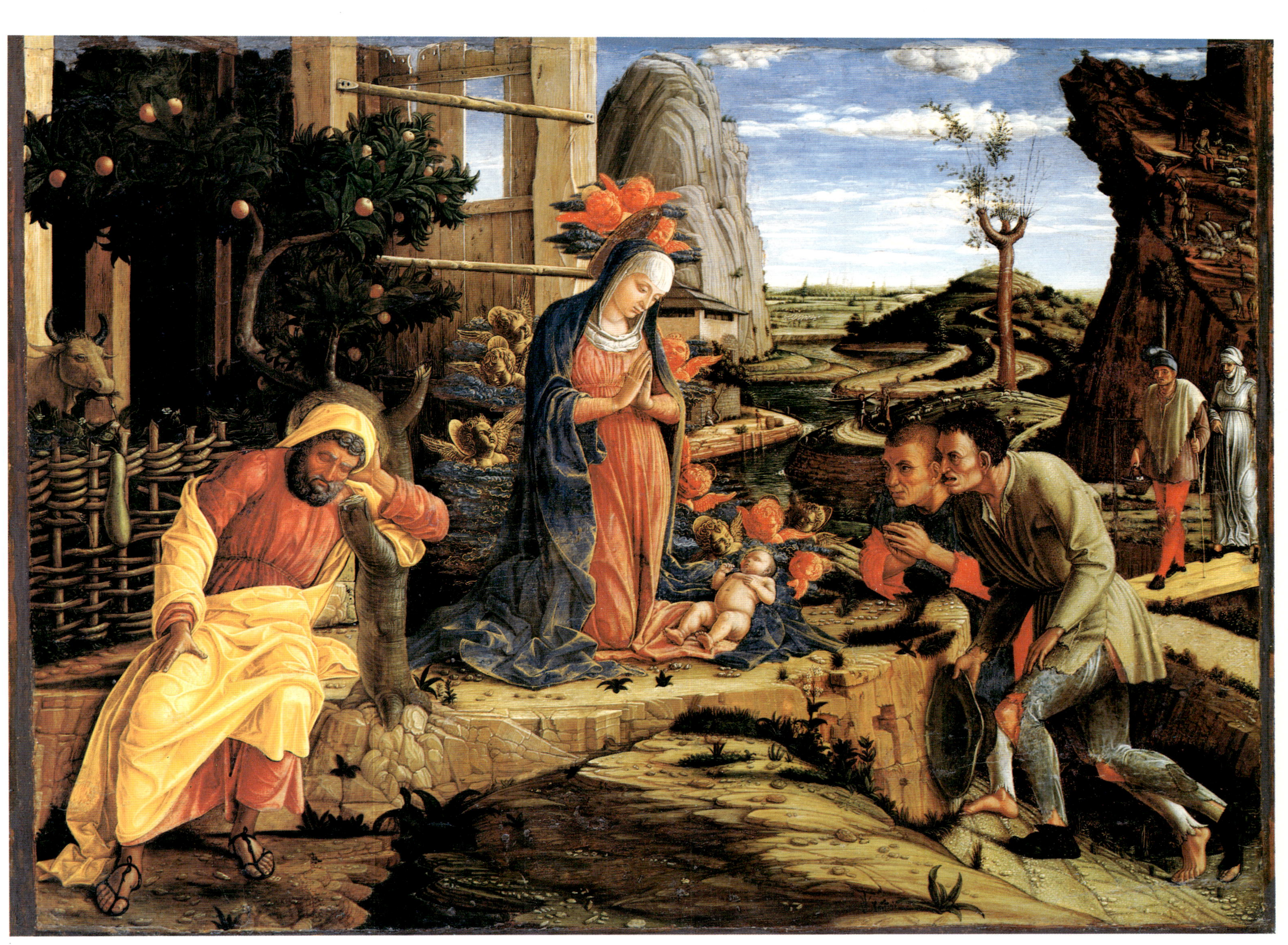

Raphael (RAFFAELLO SANZIO), 1483–1520, *Italian*

MADONNA AND CHILD ENTHRONED WITH SAINTS (c. 1505)

RAPHAEL PAINTED THIS ALTAR in Perugia for the nuns of Sant' Antonio di Padova, who had to sell it piece by piece about one hundred and fifty years later. It is now the only Raphael altarpiece outside Europe. Most of the painting is in the clear, delicate, and balanced manner of Raphael's master Perugino. But perhaps after he laid out the painting, a visit to Florence showed him the new massive and simple figures that the High Renaissance had adopted from Masaccio. So Raphael painted the two male saints to the right and left with this solidity that prevailed outside his provincial Perugia. The Metropolitan also owns one of the five little panels that composed the predella under the big painting. Being at eye level, predella panels invite intimate inspection, and being inconspicuous, they encouraged a painter to dare new effects. And indeed, the little painting of the *Agony in the Garden* (on this page) shows none of the bright, old-fashioned colors of the Madonna; it is in the twilight browns that Leonardo da Vinci was bringing into fashion in Florence. The *Madonna* and the *Agony in the Garden* look like the work of two different painters in two different epochs. Raphael needed but to glance at a painting in order to absorb its style into his practice.

Tempera, oil, and gold on wood
Main panel 66¾ × 66½″
Lunette 25½ × 67½″
Gift of J. Pierpont Morgan, 1916

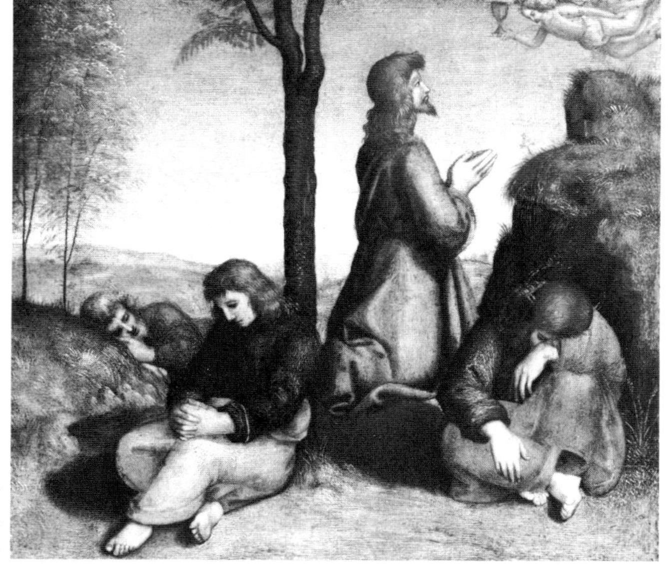

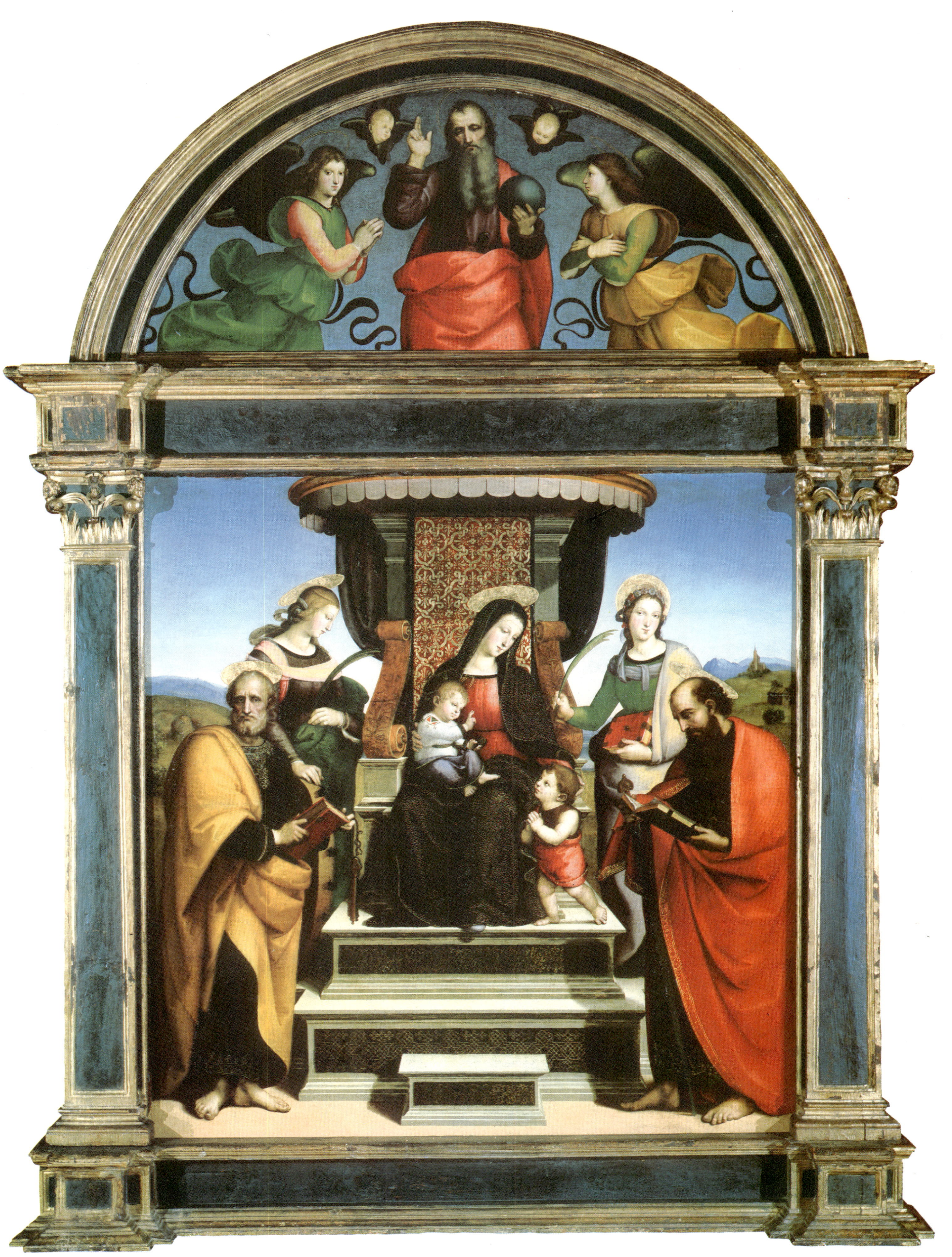

Titian (TIZIANO VECELLI), c. 1488–1576, *Italian*

VENUS AND THE LUTE PLAYER (c. 1560–65)

THE SUBJECT SEEMS TO BE ONE that Renaissance Italians delighted in debating: Does beauty enter the soul more through the ear or the eye? Such an academic speculation required a sensuality as massive as Titian's to generate a great work of art. He painted half a dozen variations of this picture before coming to this final one when he was in his seventies. The blurring of his eyesight, like old Degas's, broadened his touch to summarize details in a large design. The landscape, a memory of bygone afternoons among faraway hills, is as much a reverie as the soft woman adrift in daydreams. Where other artists deliver passion, grandeur, action, wit, eccentricity, realism, virtuosity, brutality, or mystical vision, Titian alone soared into a sumptuousness of beauty that has made him almost the only artist whose desirability has never for one moment declined.

Oil on canvas 65 × 82½"
Munsey Fund, 1936

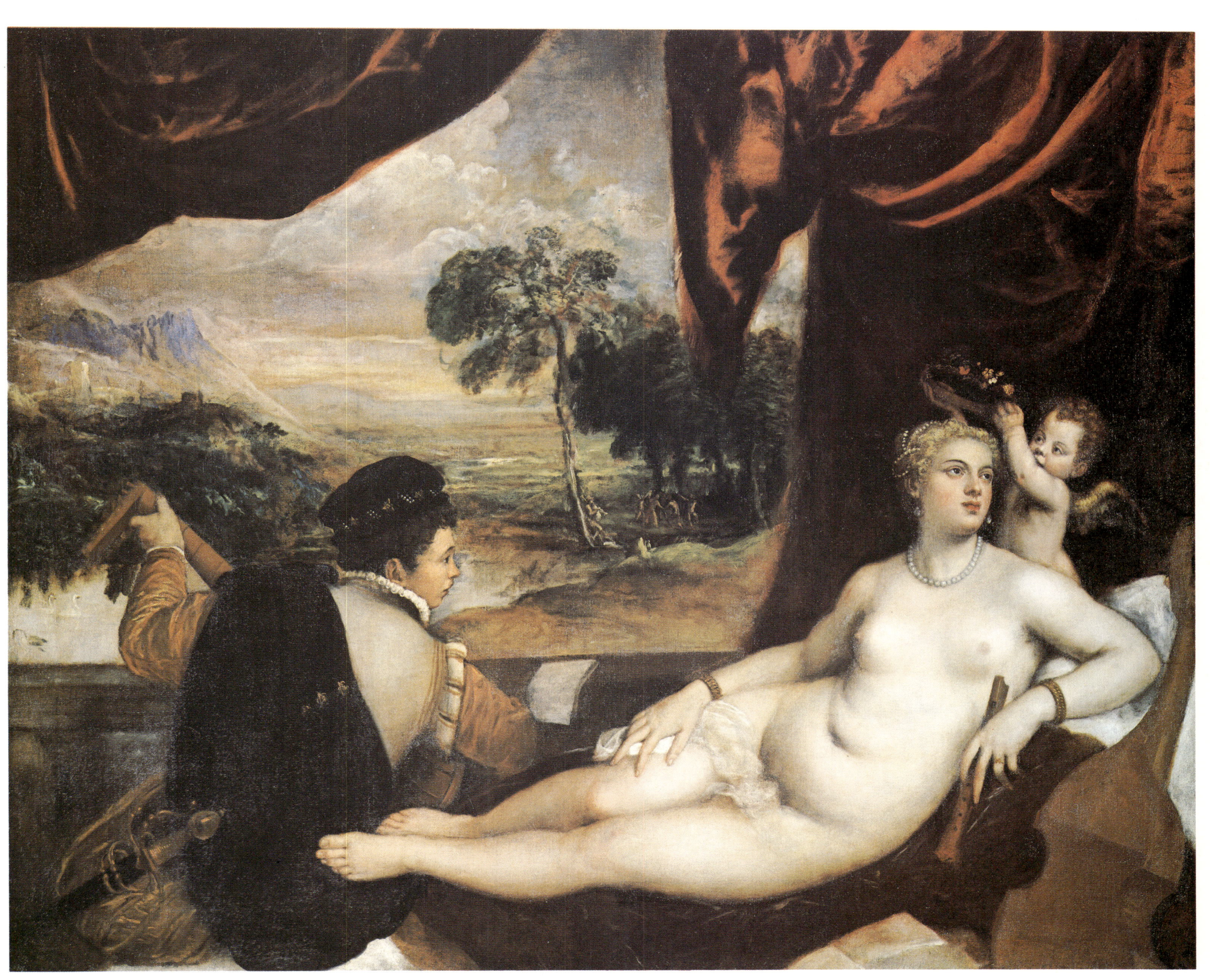

Veronese (PAOLO CALIARI), 1528–1588, *Italian*

MARS AND VENUS UNITED BY LOVE (c. 1570–80)

VERONESE'S SCULPTOR FATHER trained him as a boy to a grasp of form. When he turned to painting, he learned to invent drapery (now a lost art) by studying Dürer's prints, and he adapted noble attitudes from Parmigiano's etchings. He worked in and around Verona until, in his late twenties, he began the extensive decorations of San Sebastiano in Venice, which won him Venetian commissions for the rest of his life. When he was thirty-five, he filled the end of the huge refectory of San Giorgio Maggiore with the vast *Marriage at Cana*, later taken by Napoleon to the Louvre. This made such a sensation that he painted five more pictures of splendid feasts. As one of the leading painters in Venice, he shared in the redecorating of the Doge's Palace after it was gutted by fire in 1574. He accomplished this huge amount of work by organizing a team of his two sons, his brother, and Battista Zelotti, who specialized in the architectural backgrounds that hold groups of figures together. Veronese did not paint individuals, but inaccessibly regal types of queens and princes. He became Tiepolo's model for the grand gesture and the imaginative extravagance of costume.

Oil on canvas 81 × 63⅜"
John Stewart Kennedy Fund, 1910

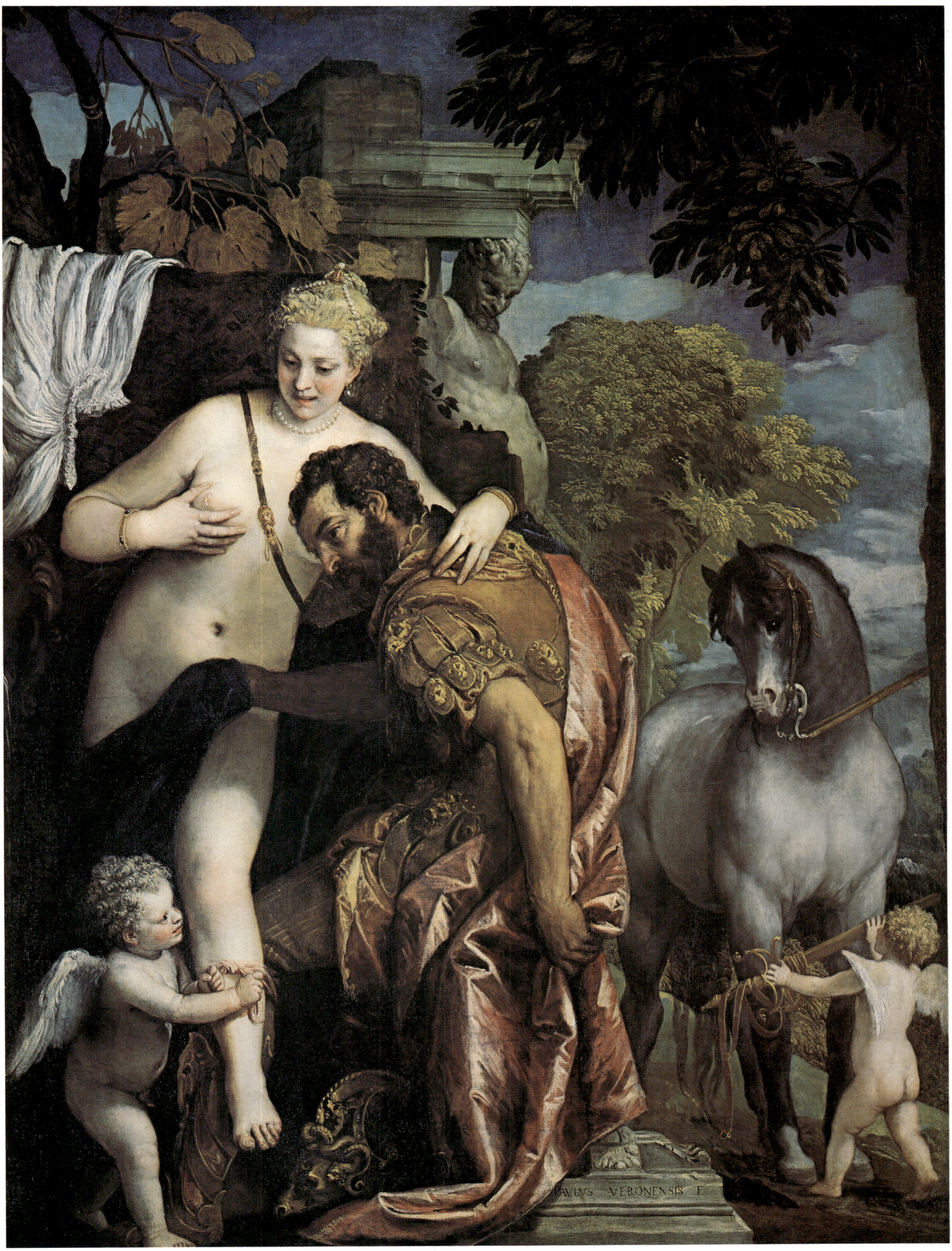
PAVLVS VERONENSIS F

Bronzino (AGNOLO DI COSIMO DI MARIANO), 1503–1572, *Italian*

PORTRAIT OF A YOUNG MAN

IN 1532 THE ACQUIESCENCE of the Pope and the Emperor Charles V allowed Cosimo de' Medici to begin calling himself a grand duke when he married Eleonora of Toledo, the rich daughter of the Spanish viceroy of Naples. Among the wedding decorations, Cosimo liked some by Agnolo Bronzino so much that he commissioned the painter to do his portrait, and he followed this with some thirty portraits of Medici past and present. During this thirty-year glorification of a newly ennobled family, Bronzino developed the society portrait, which had been invented by his master, Pontormo. The aloof, impenetrable social icon was then perfected by van Dyck in Genoa and London and continued by the British portraitists to Sargent, its last authoritative master.

This portrait was engraved as a Duke of Urbino. If so, it would represent Giudobaldo II (1514–1574) who could have posed when Bronzino was in Urbino in 1530–1532. At seventeen or so, the young Duke might have relaxed in the adolescent assurance that he had done his share simply by taking the trouble to be born.

Oil on wood 37 ⅝ × 29½″
Bequest of Mrs. H. O. Havemeyer, 1929
The H. O. Havemeyer Collection

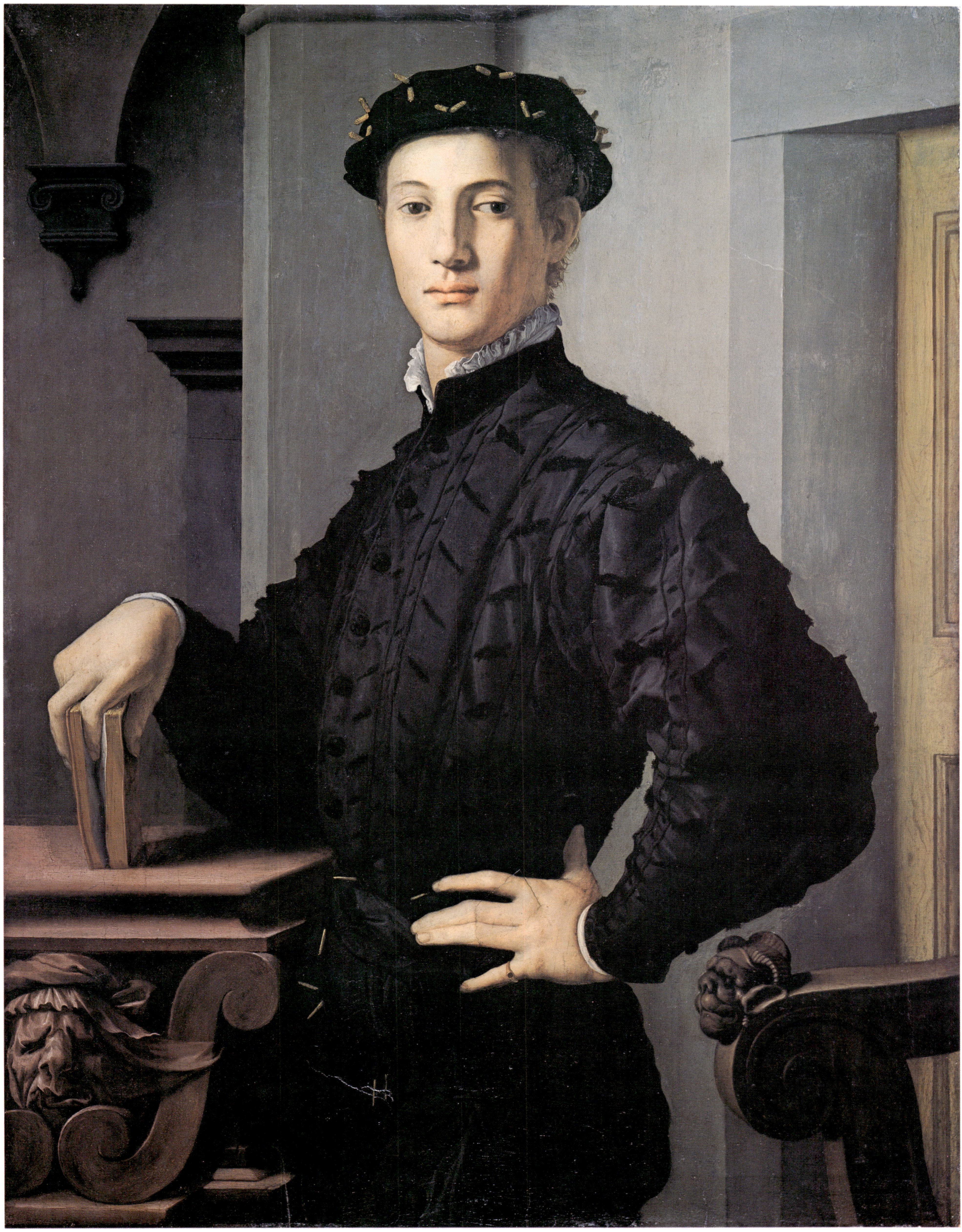

Pieter Bruegel the Elder, active by 1551, died 1569, *Flemish*

THE HARVESTERS (1565)

BRUEGEL MADE MANY PEN DRAWINGS that Antwerp engravers reproduced and shipped out to the Old and New Worlds. Only in the last decade of his rather short life does he seem to have painted. By then he had learned from Italian art to draw figures roundly and moving in every possible action; but instead of drawing nudes with drapery thrown over them, as the Italians did, he fitted bodies with clothes that usage has stretched into a distinguishing skin. Though he was probably born of peasants and kept up with village weddings, carnivals, and wakes, he studied these country matters with the relish of a city intellectual plunging into a change of scene. This panel represents July in a series of the months. The *Months*, along with most of Bruegel's painted work, once belonged to Rudolph II in Prague, whose collection largely survives in Vienna. Since most of Bruegel's paintings have always been concentrated in one gallery, they were known to relatively few people until the 1920s when Germans and Austrians published large, framable color reproductions.

Oil on wood 46½ ×63¼"
Rogers Fund, 1919

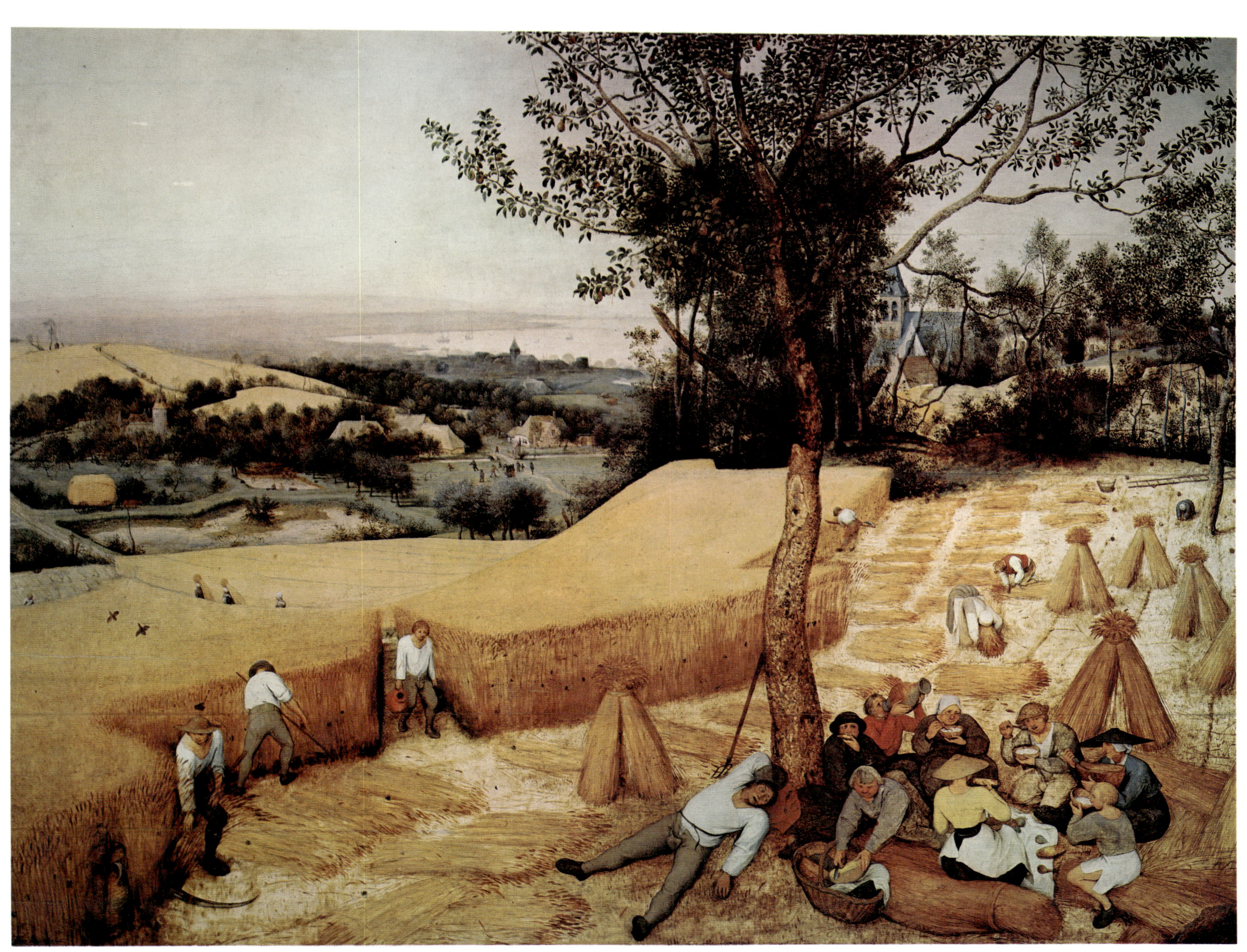

El Greco (DOMENICOS THEOTOCOPOULOS) 1541–1614, *Spanish*

VIEW OF TOLEDO (c. 1604–14)

EL GRECO HAD LEARNED THE Byzantine tradition of icon painting before he left his native Crete for Venice. In Italy he retrained under the freedom and fluidity of Venetian brushwork and Mannerism's elegant gestures in figures as tall as his stiff Byzantine saints. Then in the artistic solitude of Toledo he fused these disparate influences into his flickering evocations of miracle that exactly suited the Spanish visionaries, even though his idiosyncrasy clashed with Philip II's orthodox literalness. El Greco's training in icon painting had familiarized him with the subject of Mount Sinai, which he later painted in Italy. When he came to Toledo, he found himself on a hilltop as extraordinary as any imaginary Sinai. This vision of Toledo, with its buildings rearranged, is the most striking survivor of several views that he painted. The sky, electric with unearthly storms, must record the weather through which Moses looked up at the Lord descending with the Tablets of the Law.

Oil on canvas 47¾ × 42¾″
Bequest of Mrs. H. O. Havemeyer, 1929
The H.O. Havemeyer Collection

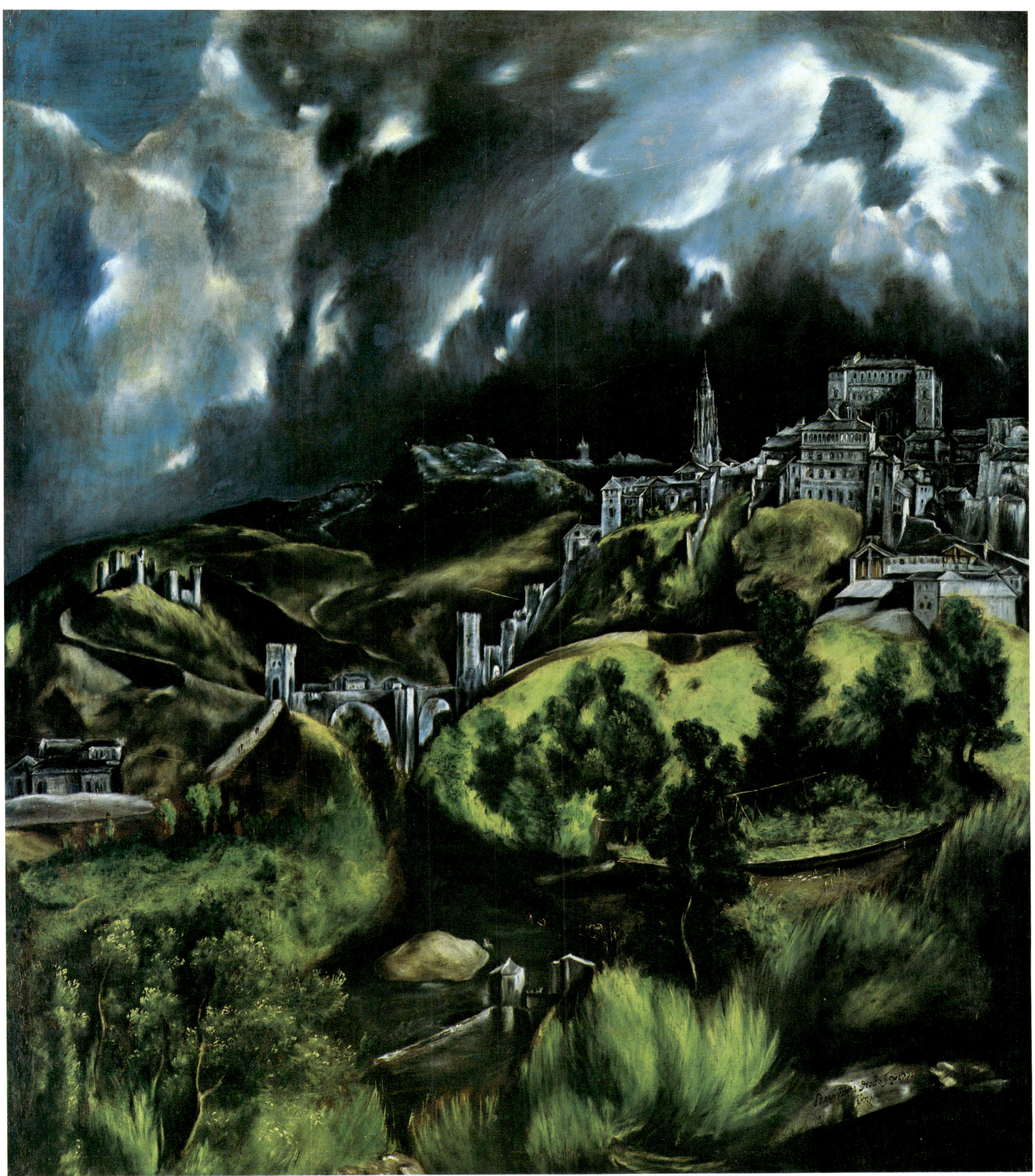

Diego Rodríguez de Silva y Velázquez, 1599–1660, *Spanish*

JUAN DE PAREJA (c. 1649–50)

IN 1650, WHILE IN Rome to buy pictures and sculpture for the king of Spain, Velázquez was commissioned to paint Pope Innocent X. Since he had not held a brush for some time, he got back into practice with this portrait of his Moorish assistant, who was also a painter. The portrait made a sensation. When the sitter exhibited it on March 19, 1650, it was said that no one knew which one to speak to or which one would answer. Velázquez for once was painting someone he knew intimately and did not have to flatter. He charged the head with menace by displacing it to left of center, an asymmetrical layout that was later made to conform to Italian norms by folding the canvas under at the right and at the top. The Museum has restored the original spacing. Velázquez organized the features around the striking interplay of arched eyebrows and mustache springing inside the tight oval of the face. In every head he always discovered an individual geometry that stamps each portrait with a haunting uniqueness.

Oil on canvas. 32 × 27½″
Fletcher Fund, Rogers Fund, and Bequest of Miss Adelaide Milton de Groot (1876–1967), by exchange, supplemented by gifts from friends of the Museum, 1971

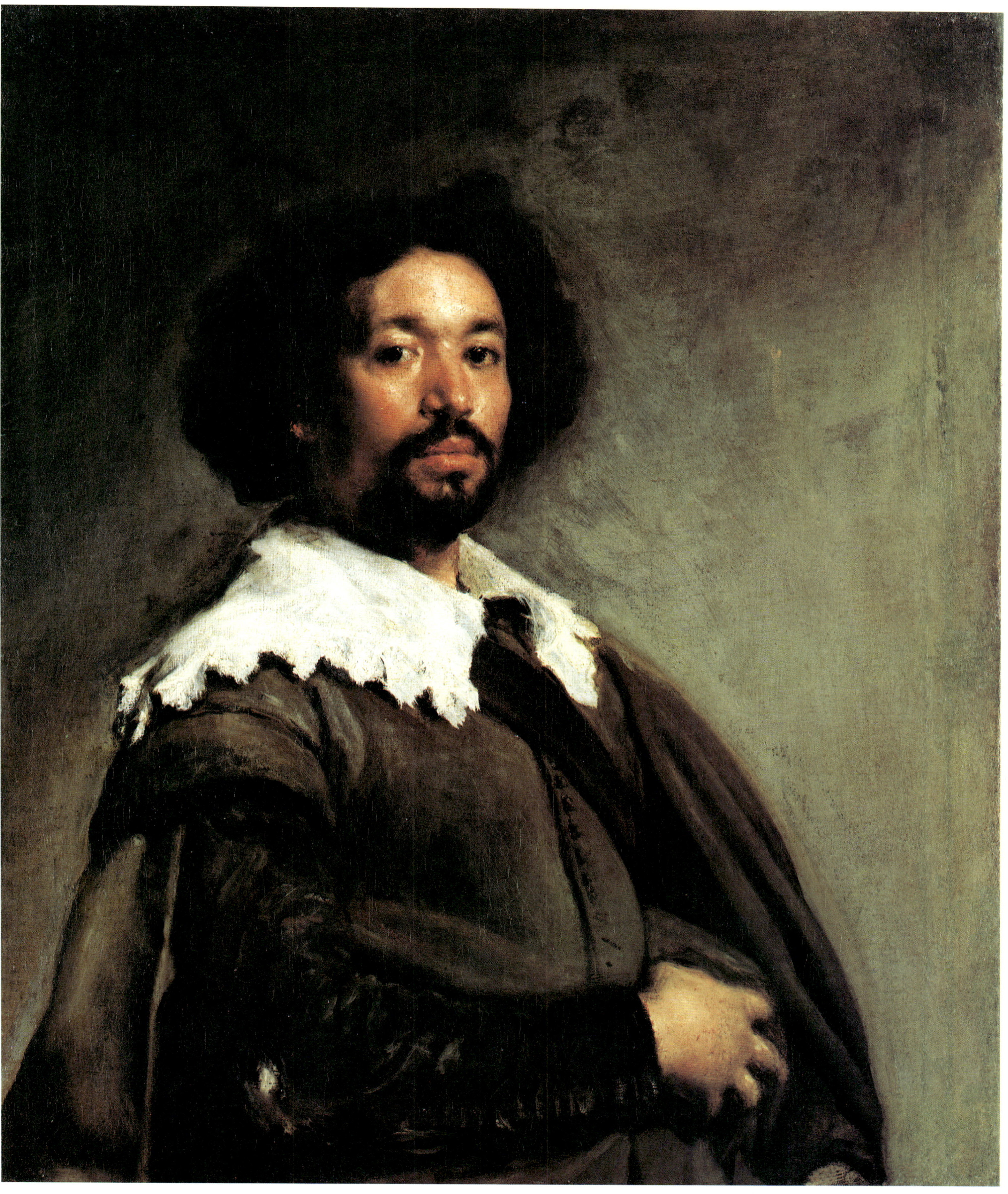

Peter Paul Rubens (and WORKSHOP), 1577–1640, *Flemish*

WOLF AND FOX HUNT

FROM 1615 TO 1621 Rubens painted several large hunts to decorate the palaces of princes who hunted with an often obsessive passion. Machiavelli urged rulers to hunt for healthy exercise away from court intrigues and for a chance to study where to deploy their soldiers for possible battles. In these pictures Rubens followed an accepted artistic practice by inventing the composition and then hiring specialist painters to execute the animals, flowers, landscapes, or architecture. He himself would have painted the heads of the hunters and would have touched up the whole to unify it, rather the way an architectural firm operates today. To impose his personality through delegated work, a painter had to establish a bold and clear design for a crew who all shared a common taste and technique. Such coordinated effort became impossible after about 1800 when painters developed highly individual styles. Degas, for instance, his eye trained by the Italian Renaissance, designed ruggedly enough to survive execution by others had he not felt that design and execution fused in one action. Renoir, without such intellectual discipline, relied solely on the personal touch of his brush and usually designed too feebly to work through others even if he had wanted to try.

Oil on canvas. 96⅝ × 148⅛″
John Stewart Kennedy Fund, 1910

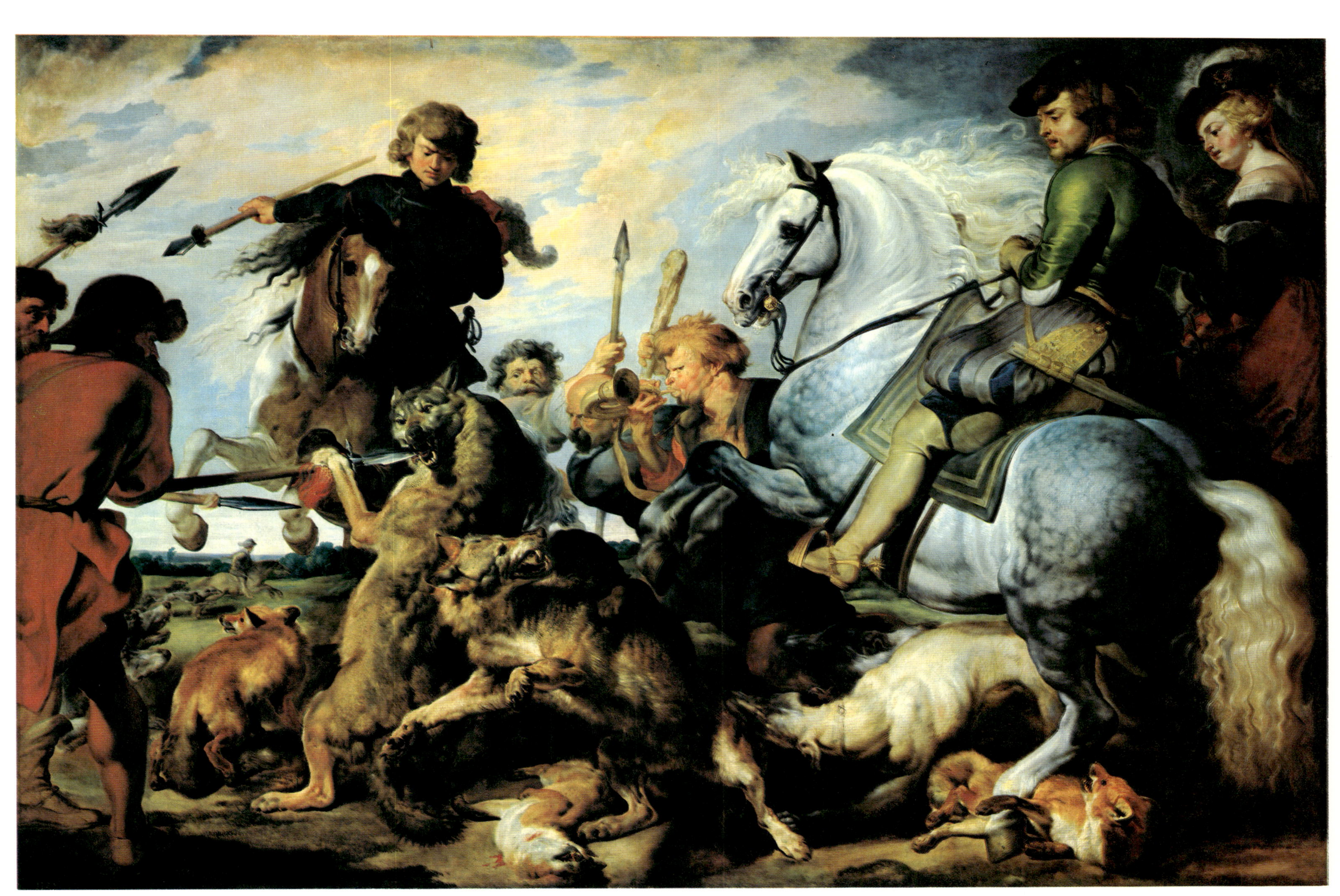

Anthony van Dyck, 1599–1641, *Flemish*

JAMES STUART, DUKE OF RICHMOND AND LENNOX (c. 1632–34)

Van Dyck made a masterpiece of easy elegance by diminishing the duke's head, stretching his body, and subduing all colors to the honey gloss of his curling locks. We look up at him from the level of his yearning hound, as though we were a courtier bowing low. When, at twelve, James Stuart became a duke on the death of his father, he was made the ward of his nearest relative, King James I. He traveled in Italy, France, and Spain, where Philip IV created him a grandee at twenty. He was Charles I's favorite cousin, and he lent the king £66,000 to help him fight against Cromwell. The duke, as a man of fashion, wears knit silk stockings in several layers, wrinkling over each other. This was almost a necessity in freezing palace halls.

Oil on canvas. 85 × 50¼″
Gift of Henry G. Marquand, 1889
Marquand Collection

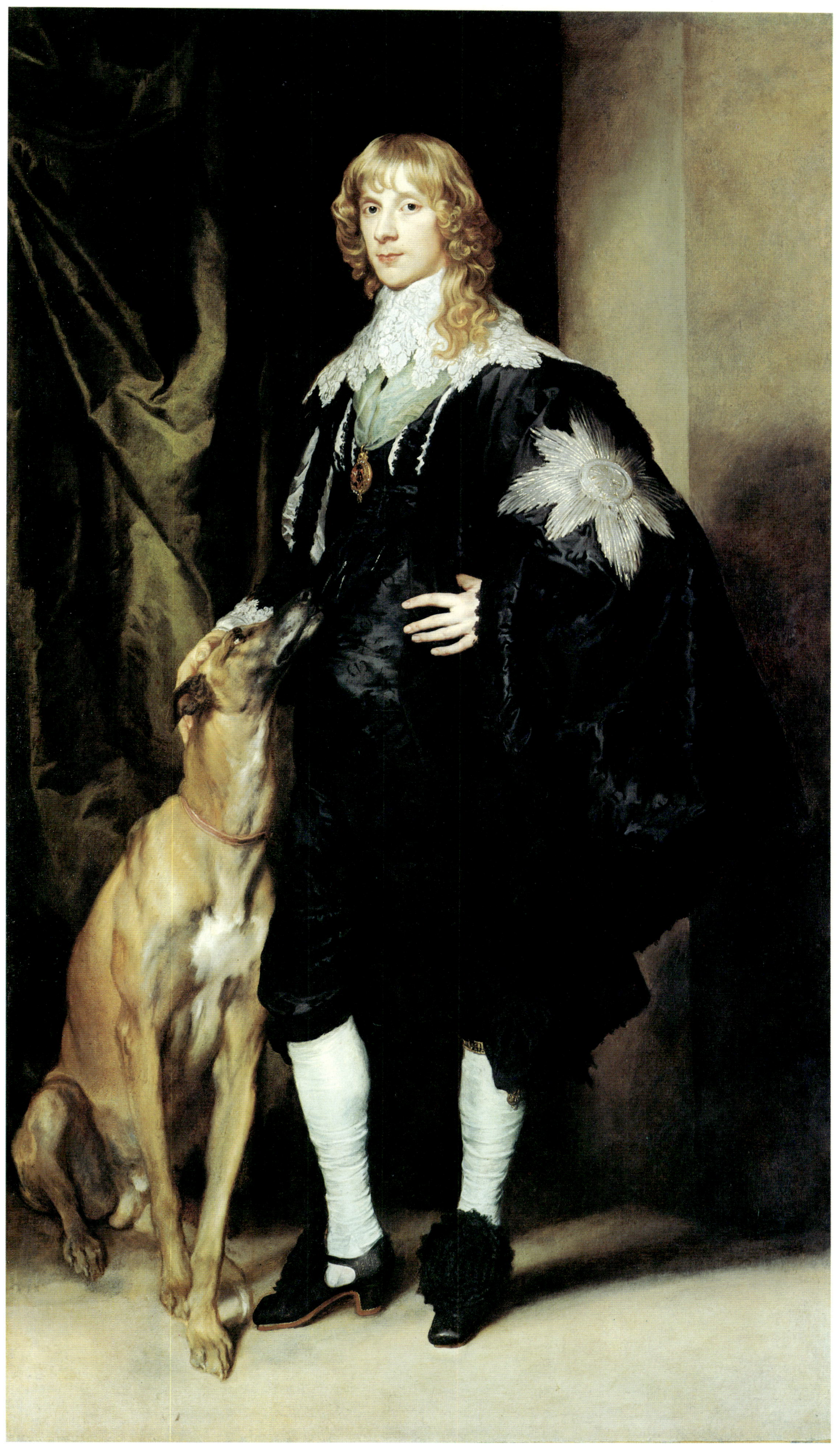

Frans Hals, c. 1580–1666, *Dutch*

MERRYMAKERS AT SHROVETIDE (c. 1616)

THE DUTCH ATE AND DRANK with abandon on the Sunday, Monday, and Tuesday before they started to fast for the forty days of Lent. The two men garlanded with food are masquerading as Pickled Herring and Hans Wurst (Sausage) for the mock battle against Lent. For centuries the North Sea herring preserved the Dutch from the famines that starved to death thousands of Frenchmen and Germans. Holland enjoyed a prosperity that Louis XIV and Colbert could neither ignore nor forgive. When the Dutch took such justified pride in their sturdy fishing and trading ships, their astuteness in business, their farms recovered from the sea bottom, and the magnanimity of their religious tolerance, it is no wonder that they so often painted themselves fat and sassy. Hals made this exuberant picture in his youth, before he had discovered how to slash paint in the brusque, segregated brushstrokes that were to be emulated by Sargent, Boldini, and Zorn.

Oil on canvas. 51¾ × 39¼"
Bequest of Benjamin Altman, 1913

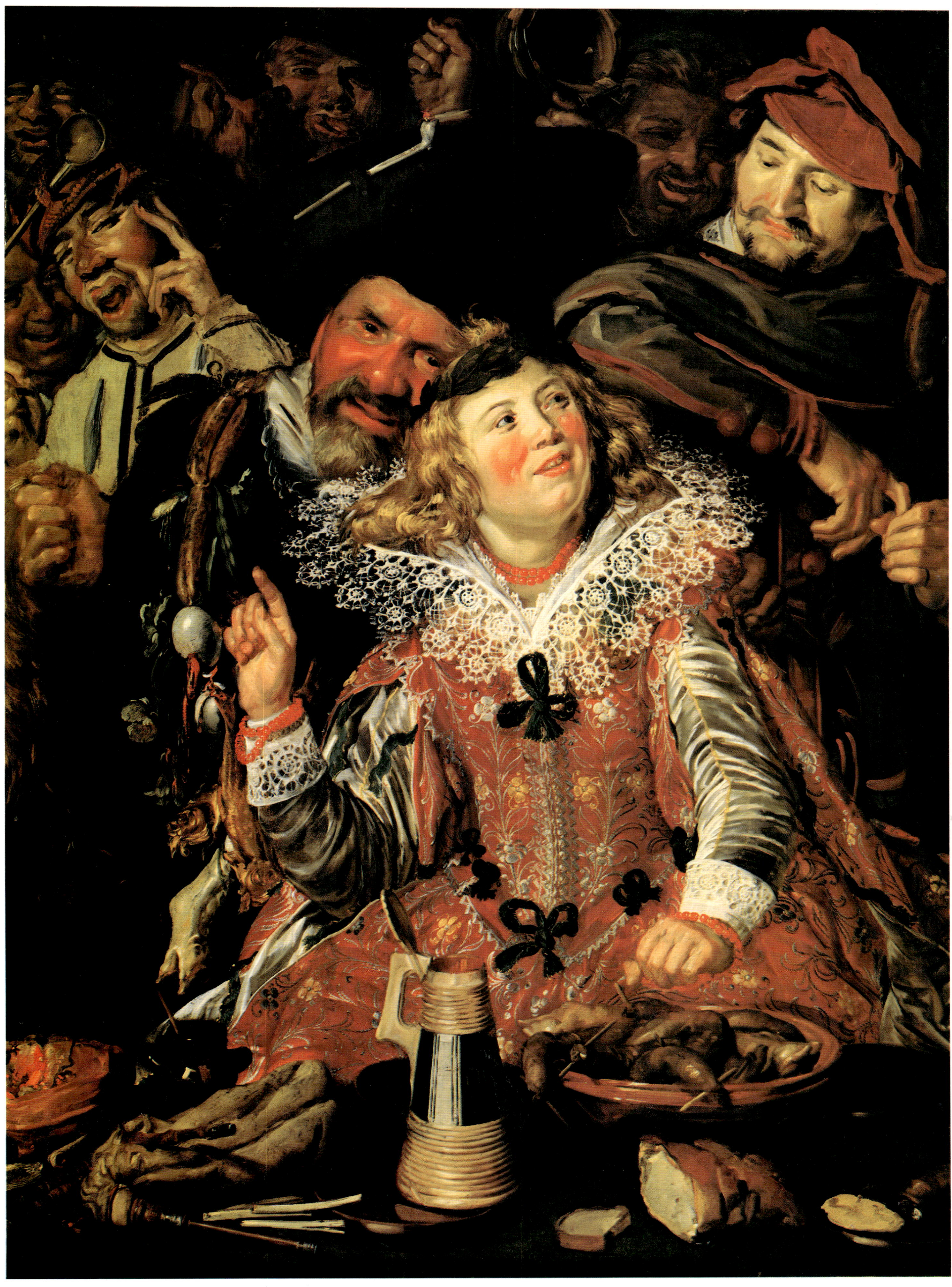

Rembrandt Harmensz. van Rijn, 1606–1669, *Dutch*

ARISTOTLE WITH A BUST OF HOMER (1653)

WHEN REMBRANDT WAS forty-seven and was etching his greatest biblical subjects, he painted this picture for Don Antonio Ruffo in Messina. The Sicilian inventory lists it as "Aristotle placing one hand on a statue." Without this identification no one today would guess at Aristotle, though everyone would recognize the "statue" as a plaster cast of an antique head of Homer. Ruffo must have dictated this literary subject, for Rembrandt probably never read Homer and certainly knew nothing about Aristotle. But in these magical years Rembrandt gave life to whatever he touched. He put thought into the ink-sparkle of the eye. He did not paint mere lips but the inside of the speaking, breathing mouth. And he managed the coarse-ground white-lead paint—as rebellious to the brush as soft putty—so that it spread in glowing crumbles on Aristotle's flowing sleeves.

Oil on canvas 56½ × 53¾"
Purchased with special funds and gifts of friends of the Museum, 1961

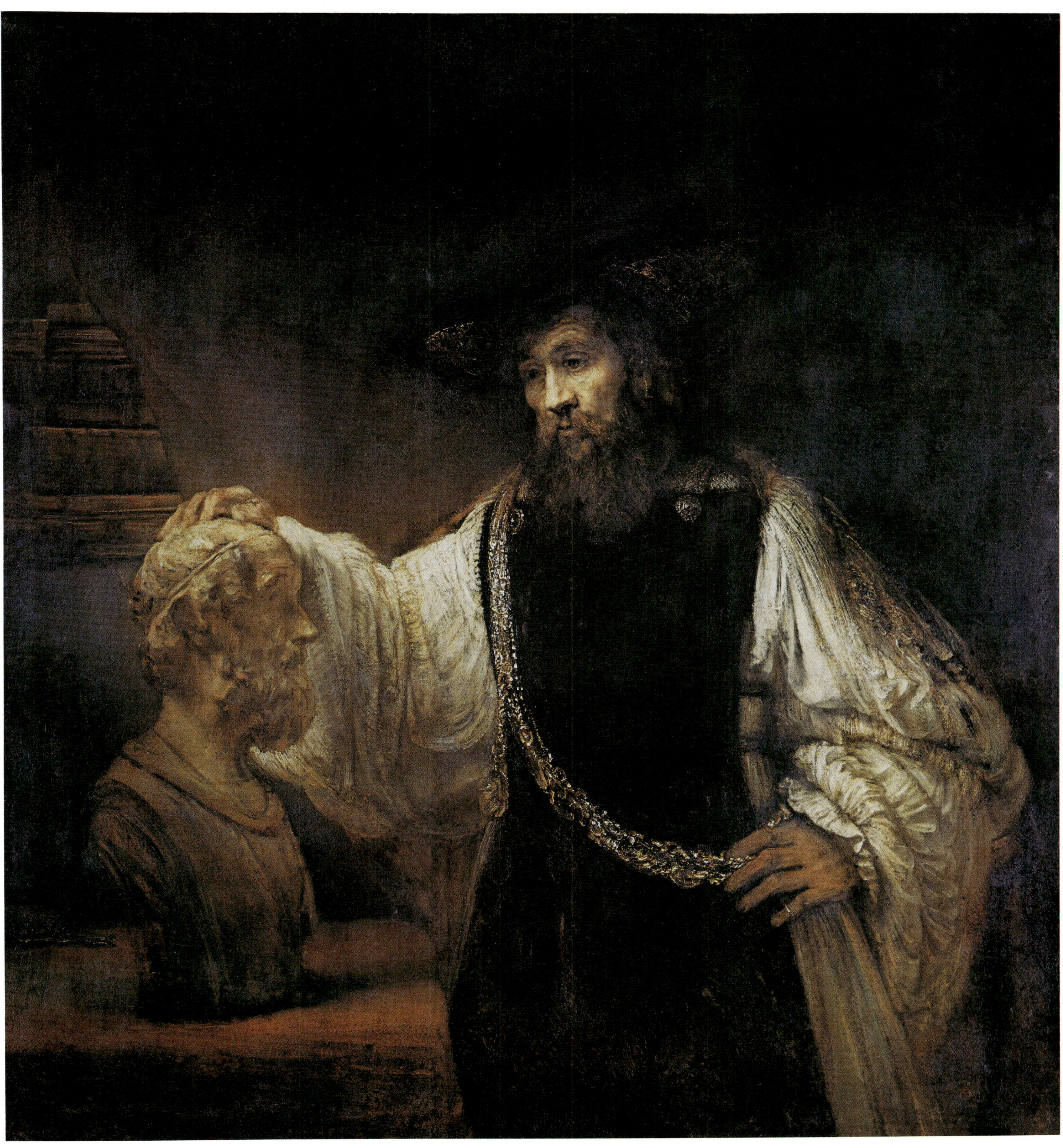

Rembrandt Harmensz. van Rijn, 1606–1669, *Dutch*

HENDRICKJE STOFFELS (1660)

REMBRANDT'S GREATEST ETCHED PORTRAITS represent men, but his private life depended on women. His mother, who was painted holding a Bible, must have formed his habit of going to Scripture for inspiration, while other Dutch painters ignored it. He gave his mother's name, Cornelia, to three of his daughters, of whom the first two died as infants. His marriage to Saskia when he was twenty-eight brought him a handsome fortune and a connection with art dealers of a grander family than his own. Her death after eight years left him with her only surviving child, the year-old Titus, for whom he hired a nurse, who became his mistress. By the time the nurse had to be dismissed as insane, a plump little peasant girl, Hendrickje Stoffels, had joined the household; she eventually became Rembrandt's ideal companion and helper. She signed her name with an X, but she was bright, levelheaded, and above all compassionate. He could not afford to marry her because that would have cost him the income from suspicious Saskia's dowry. When Hendrickje had been with Rembrandt for about ten years, she reorganized his affairs after his bankruptcy by setting up as an art dealer in partnership with Titus, then seventeen. They relieved Rembrandt of all financial responsibility by hiring him to work for the firm. Hendrickje's death about two years after this portrait was painted must have caused Rembrandt's darkest hour. He painted her with a tenderness, an intimacy, that make our examination of her portrait an invasion of privacy.

Oil on canvas 30⅞ × 27⅛″
Gift of Archer M. Huntington in memory of
his father Collis Potter Huntington, 1926

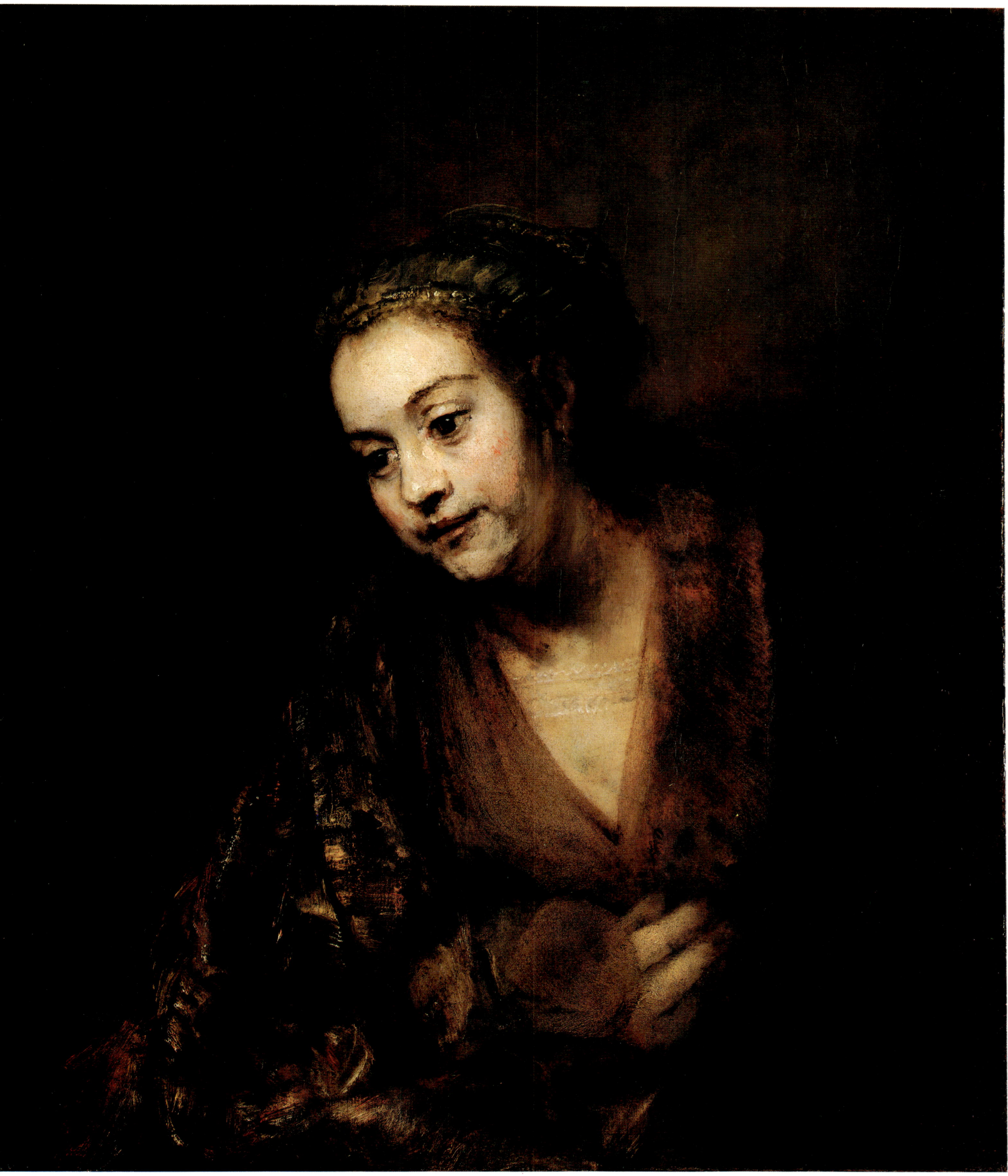

Johannes Vermeer, 1632–1675, *Dutch*

YOUNG WOMAN WITH A WATER JUG (c. 1660)

THIS SINGULAR ARTIST FORMED his style more or less on his own, painted a small number of pictures on a very few subjects, and died at forty-three, leaving no followers. He seems to have supported his wife and eleven children more by dealing in works of art than by selling his own paintings. He may have kept much of his work to himself, for some twenty years after his death an Amsterdam auction dispersed a lot of twenty-one of his pictures, of which about fifteen can now be identified. Few men appear in the three-dozen paintings now attributed to Vermeer; nineteen represent single women, and three more a mistress and her maid. In a few rooms of his house, against a side light exquisitely sliding across a white wall, he grouped expensive furniture, musical instruments, several wall maps, and many paintings, all probably selected from his dealer's stock. He must have studied his subjects in the image that a lens casts on the ground glass of a camera obscura, coagulating bright objects into globules of halation. Vermeer's art balances all elements in a harmony of silence.

Oil on canvas 18 × 16″
Gift of Henry G. Marquand, 1889
Marquand Collection

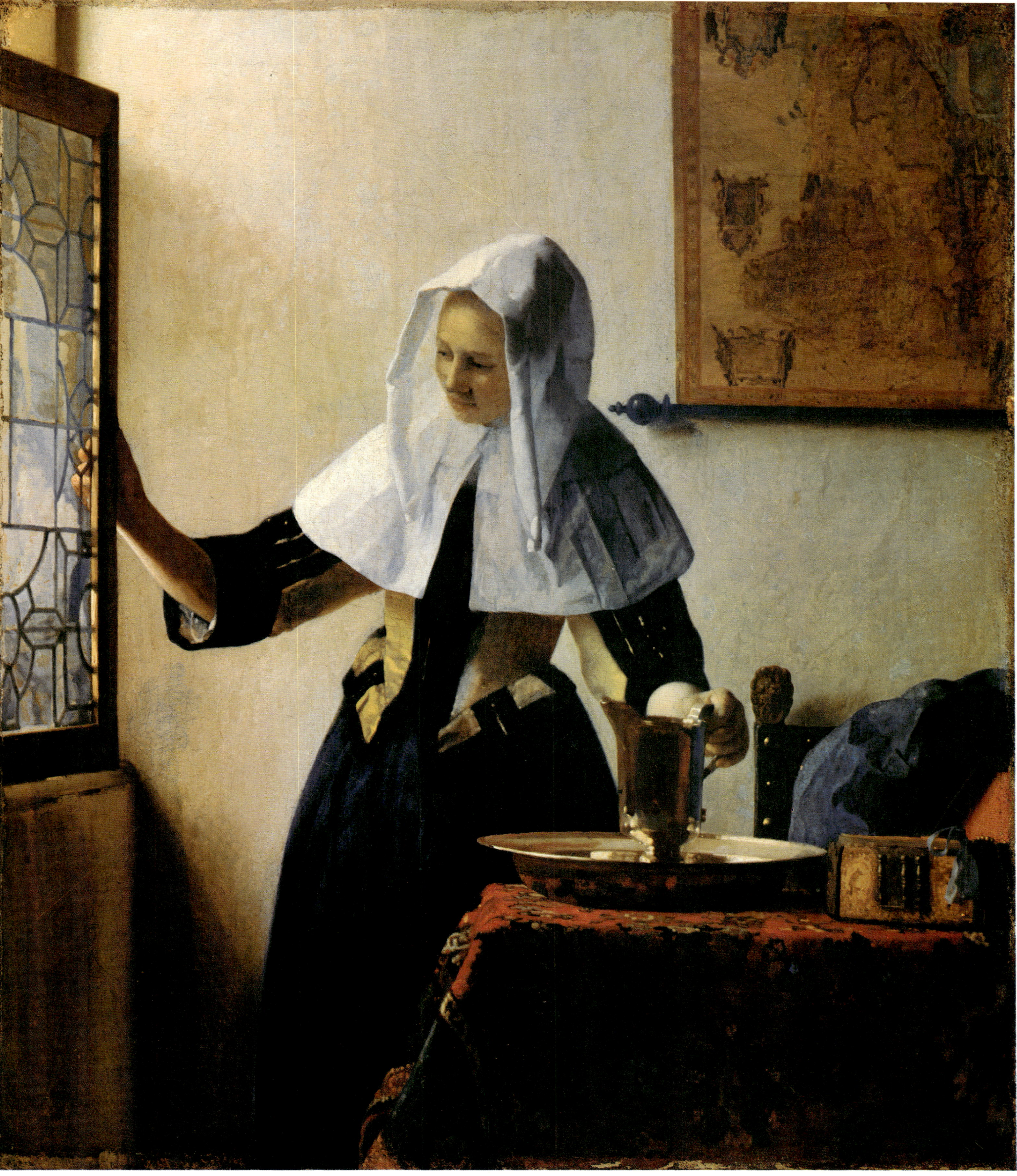

Jean-Antoine Watteau, 1684–1721, *French*

MEZZENTIN (c. 1717–19)

BY WATTEAU'S TIME Frenchmen had been laughing for well over a century at the wit of Italian troupes of players—the *Commedia dell'Arte*—so called because they had developed the art of improvising dialogue for any plot that might be given them. Watteau owned the costumes that distinguished the various stock *commedia* characters; and he dressed his friends in these costumes to paint them as actors in poetic landscapes that have nothing to do with stage scenery. The actor who always played the *mezzetin (mezzetto* is a measure of wine) was identified by his striped suit, the way a butler is distinguished by his striped waistcoat. The *mezzetin* was a shiftless, likeable lackey with a good voice, but luckless in love. Watteau painted this picture at the end of his thirty-seven years of life. After his death it went with a lot of forty of his paintings to Catherine the Great and remained in Russia until the Metropolitan Museum bought it in 1934. The Museum also owns Watteau's red-and-black chalk study for the head.

Oil on canvas 21¾ × 17″
Munsey Fund, 1934

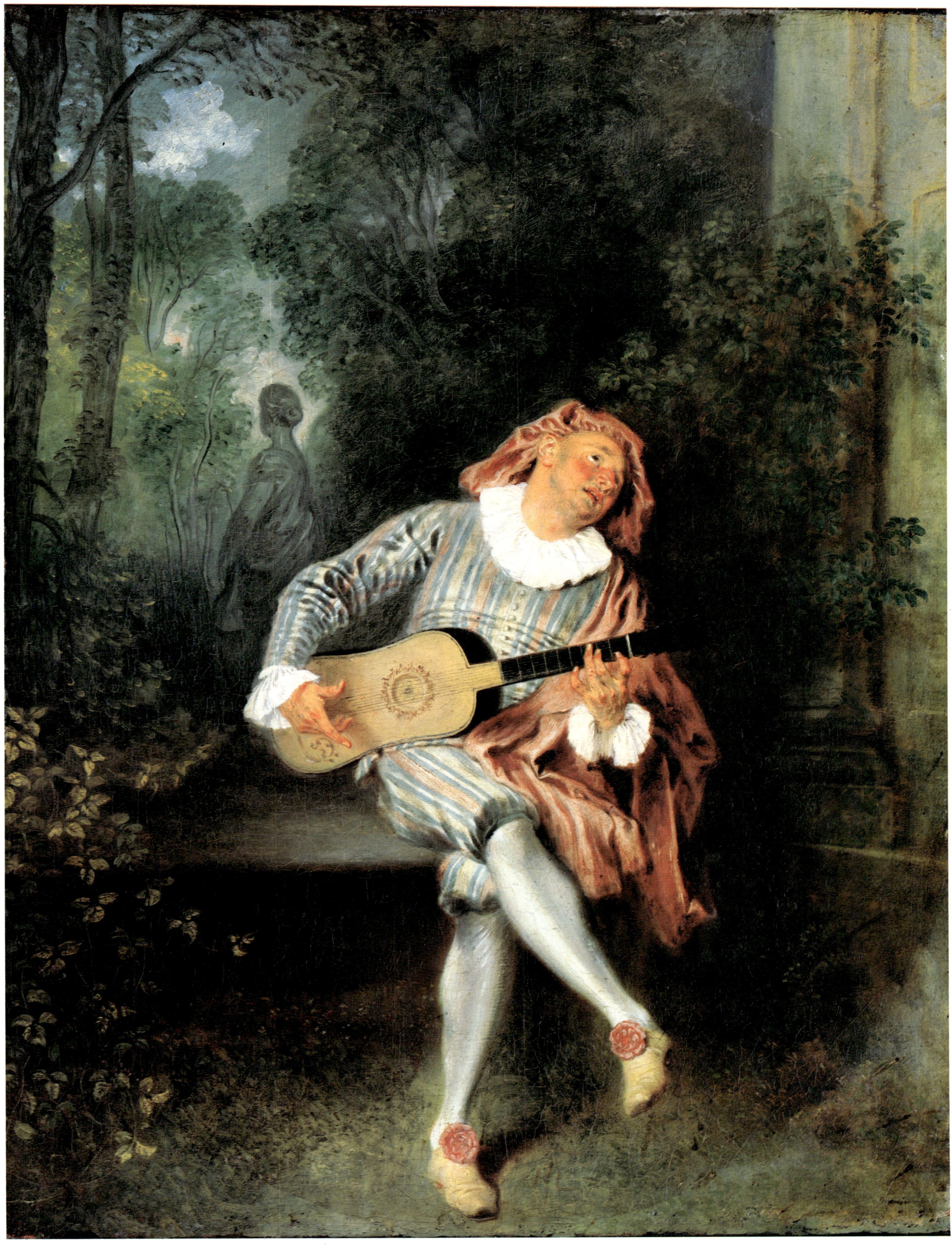

François Boucher, 1703–1770, *French*

THE TOILET OF VENUS (1751)

BOUCHER PROBABLY PAINTED THIS PICTURE for Madame de Pompadour's bathroom in her new Château de Bellevue, now destroyed. During her years as Louis XV's reigning mistress, from a little before 1750 until her early death in 1764, she encouraged the best French artists. She recognized the skill that Boucher had acquired by etching copies of some one hundred twenty-five Watteau drawings and by a short stay in Rome, where he dismayed the proper connoisseurs by calling Raphael's Madonnas insipid and Michelangelo's athletes hunch-backed, while admiring Albani for his grace and Pietro da Cortona for the smooth force of his drawing. Boucher managed to be better than a mere purveyor of luxury articles because he had mastered the skills of the High Baroque and could draw brilliantly. Over a thousand engraved copies of his works propagated his art throughout the world and made him the most influential of the rococo painters.

Oil on canvas 42⅝ × 33½″
Bequest of William K. Vanderbilt, 1920

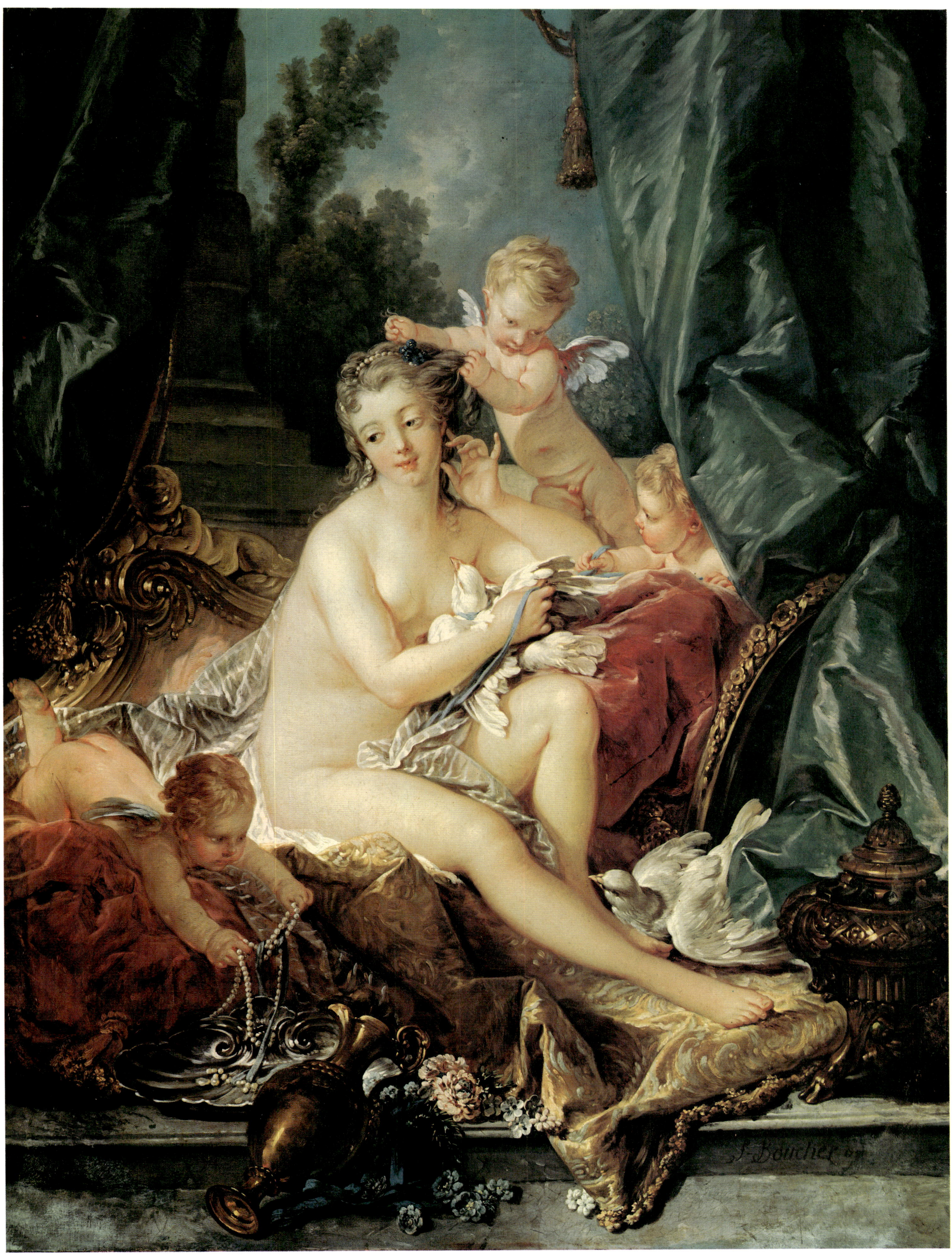

Jean-Baptiste Siméon Chardin, 1699–1779, *French*

BOY BLOWING BUBBLES

An eighteenth-century observer would at once have recognized this picture of a bubble as an allegory of the frailty and evanescence of human life. Such sober thoughts were not for the French court, which neglected this remarkably independent artist. But Chardin had a great early success with the wealthy lawyers, doctors, businessmen, and diplomats of Paris, and even of Stockholm and Glasgow. He seems to have made no drawings, but painted very deliberately, going over and over with tiny touches that build up an ember of colors. Colors reflect into each other for a unity that does not allow the bubble in this picture to stand out as a glassy climax, the way it would have done in any Dutch painting. Napoleonic grandeur snubbed Chardin's kitchen pots and sober children, but his popularity has steadily grown since about 1850. Van Gogh admired his broken color as much as Rembrandt's.

Oil on canvas 24 × 24⅞"
Wentworth Fund, 1949

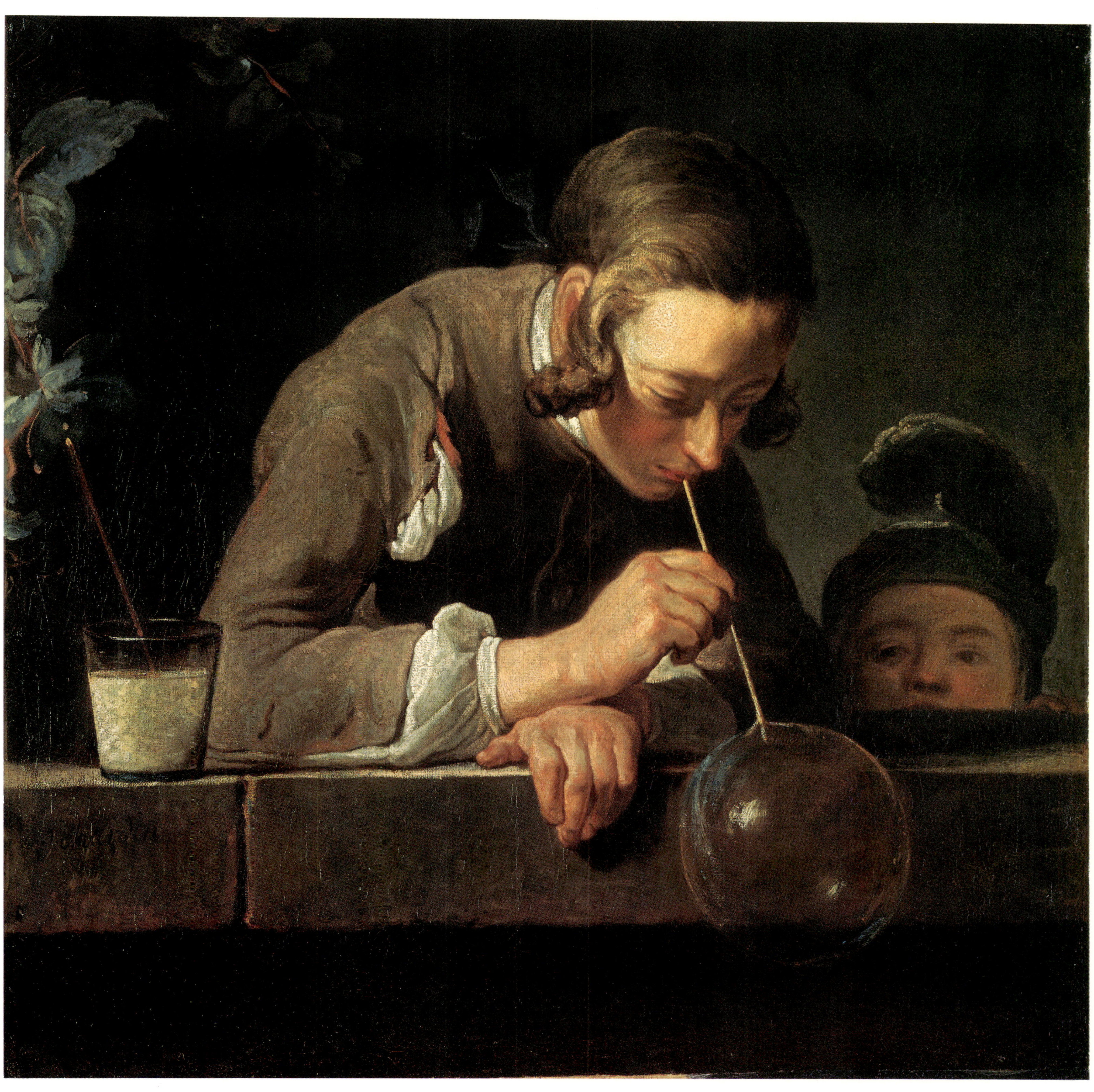

Jacques-Louis David, 1748–1825, *French*

ANTOINE-LAURENT LAVOISIER AND HIS WIFE (1789)

AFTER STUDYING SCIENCE, Lavoisier (1743–1794) improved the production of gunpowder and salt, introduced British agricultural innovations into France, regularized the confusing diversity of local French weights and measures, and planned canals and savings banks. His lasting achievement was to establish modern chemistry by drawing up the first list of elements and by analyzing the character and function of air and other gases. In the year of this portrait, he published his fundamental *Traité Elémentaire de Chimie.* He derived much of his great wealth from being a *fermier général*, one of the capitalists who yearly bought the government's authorization to collect the taxes of France. These naturally disliked tax collectors were condemned to death as a group at the end of the Terror; and Lavoisier, in spite of his immense services to the state, was guillotined with the rest on May 8, 1794. In 1805 his wife (1758–1836), who had shared his work and illustrated his books, prepared his researches for publication. The intimate grandeur of this painting would alone make it one of the greatest portraits of its century, while its human associations surcharge it with a shiver of wonder.

Oil on canvas 102¼ × 76⅝"
Purchase, Mr. and Mrs. Charles Wrightsman Gift, 1977

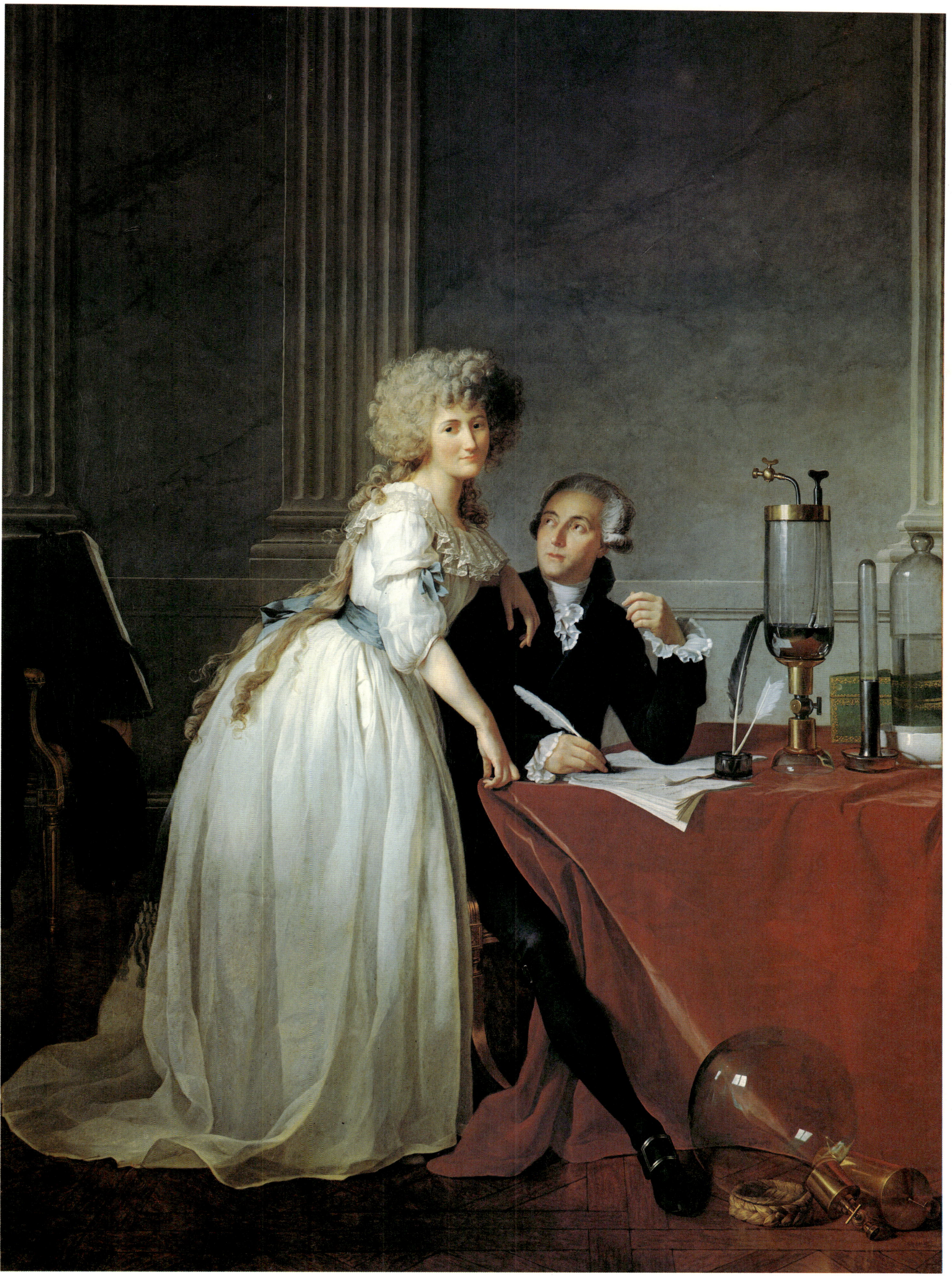

Thomas Lawrence, 1769–1830, *British*

ELIZABETH FARREN, *later* COUNTESS OF DERBY (c. 1789–90)

WILLIAM HAZLITT WAS CAPTIVATED BY Miss Farren's "fine-lady airs and graces, with the elegant turn of her head and motion of her fan and tripping of her tongue." She was born in Cork, acted in traveling troupes with her parents and sisters, and was still only fifteen when she fascinated London at the Haymarket Theatre. She retired at thirty-five to marry the Earl of Derby (founder of the Derby races)—as soon as he was freed by the death of his wife—in one of those many alliances that have maintained the vigor of the British aristocracy. This portrait of her when she was about thirty established the reputation of Lawrence, then not quite twenty-one. Old Sir Joshua Reynolds handsomely told him, "You have already achieved a masterpiece, and the world will naturally look to you to perfect that which I have endeavored to improve." Lawrence did indeed perfect the glossiest formula for society portraits, but he never again burned with the hopes and longings that sparkle in this vision of the eternal feminine.

Oil on canvas 94 × 57½″
Bequest of Edward S. Harkness, 1940

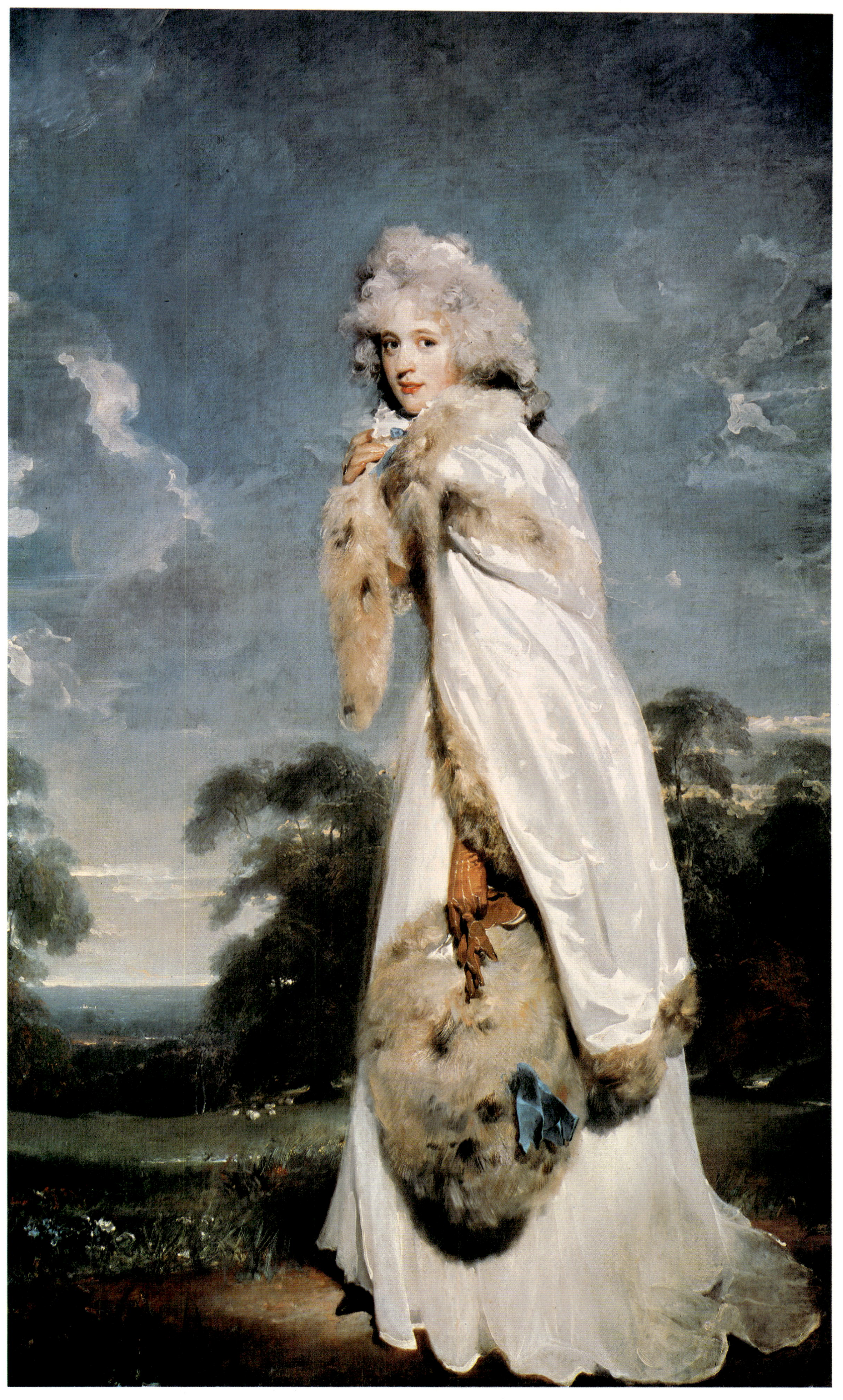

Francisco de Goya y Lucientes, 1746–1828, *Spanish*

JOSE COSTA Y BONELLS, *called* PEPITO

SPANISH PARENTS LOVE THEIR CHILDREN for what they are and hug or spank them with the confidence of instinct. This fearless naturalness cleared the way for Velázquez, Goya, and Picasso to capture the evanescent possibilities of children without prettifying them or turning them into reduced adults. Like most children, this little Pepito Costa dwindled into a nondescript adult without developing the promises that peep forth from his inquiring eyes. The boy's father was the king's doctor, and his grandfather had been the Duke of Alba's doctor. Goya portrayed many members of few families. He painted this portrait after he had refined his early patchwork of bright colors into a richer and more restricted harmony, discovering that black and white can also be colors. He mastered drawing long before he mastered color.

Oil on canvas 41⅜ × 33¼″
Gift of Countess Bismarck, 1961

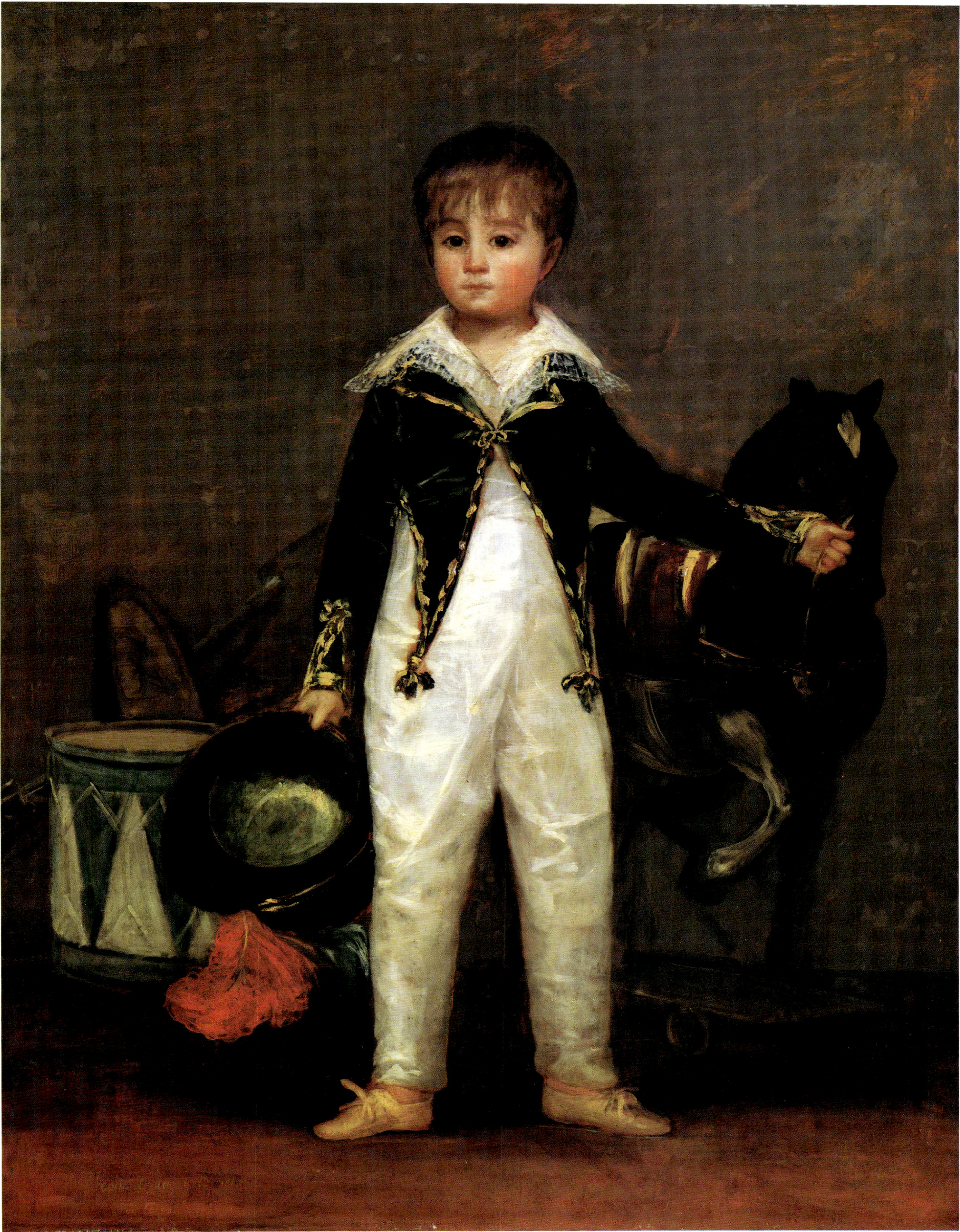

Francisco de Goya y Lucientes, 1746–1828, *Spanish*

MAJAS ON A BALCONY (c. 1810)

THE GREAT SPANISH TRADITION of the realistic novel predisposed Goya to see everyday incidents as high drama. These majas watching the life of the streets from this ordinary Madrid balcony are dashing girls of the lower or middle classes who often gathered together for a celebration on the first of May. In the late 1700s, while Marie-Antoinette was playing at being a shepherdess, the sprightlier Spanish aristocrats adopted folk dress, more or less the way young people have adopted blue jeans today. Goya painted many young dukes and duchesses dressed as majos and majas, thus emphasizing Spain's cultural independence from the domination of France. This balcony picture must have been popular, for Goya repeated it, and it inspired Manet's painting of *Le Balcon*.

Oil on canvas 76¾ × 49½″
Bequest of Mrs. H. O. Havemeyer, 1929
The H. O. Havemeyer Collection

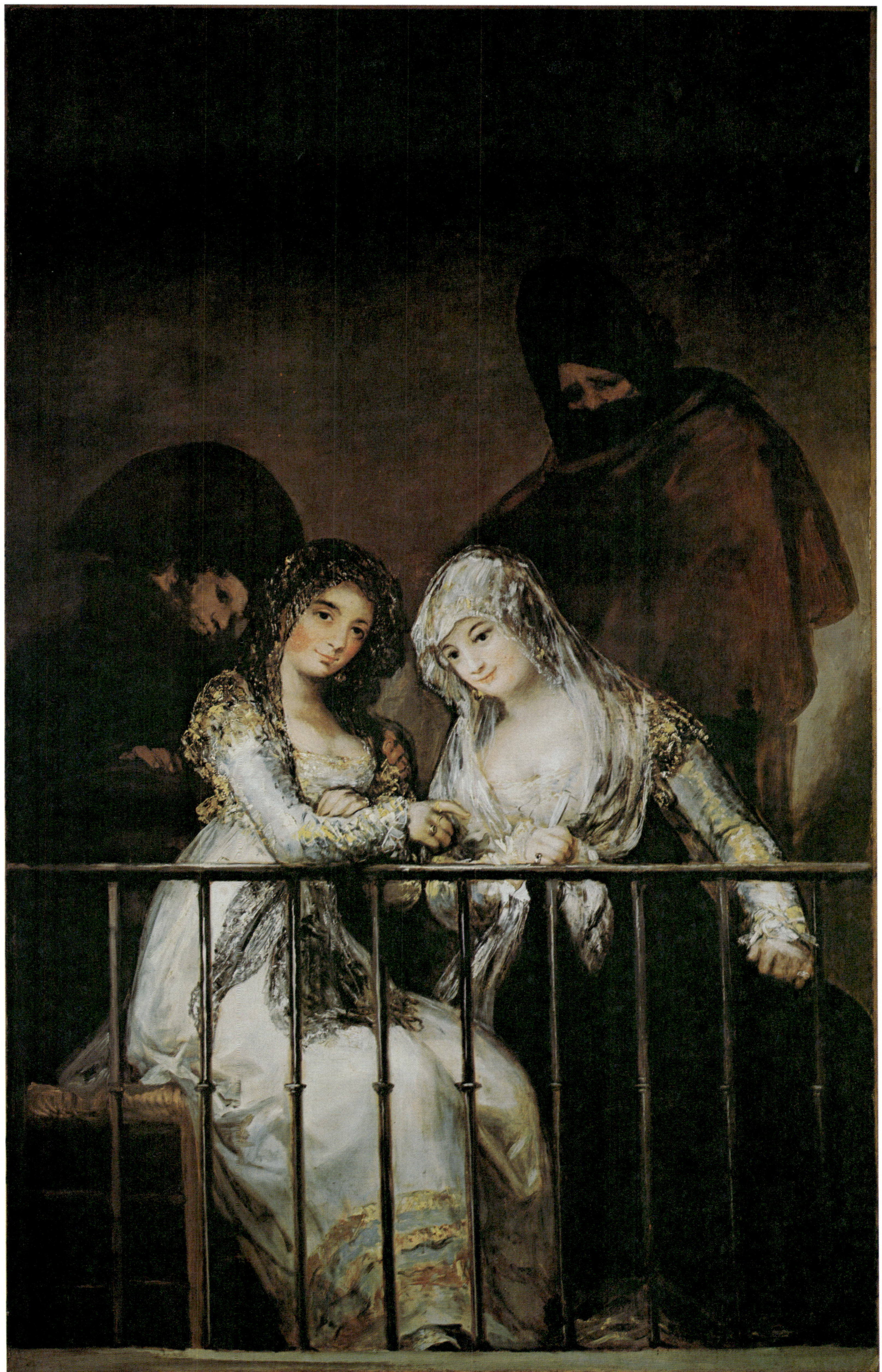

Jean-Auguste-Dominique Ingres, 1780–1867, *French*

MADAME JACQUES-LOUIS LEBLANC (1823)

INGRES PAINTED THIS LADY and her husband at the end of his sixteen years in Rome and Florence, 1808–1824. Madame Leblanc (1788–1839) had been a lady-in-waiting, and her husband, the secretary of Elisa Bacciochi, Napoleon's sister, while she was Grand Duchess of Tuscany in 1807–1809. Ingres painted the husband after only a couple of pencil studies, but he drew over twenty sketches of Françoise Leblanc, mostly of her hands and arms in tentative poses. Dodging no difficulties and leaving nothing to chance, Ingres achieved a masterpiece of exactitude that must owe something to a study of the Bronzino portraits in the Uffizi Gallery. The lady has that spice of ugliness that always fascinated Degas in any face. Degas bought this pair of portraits in 1896 at an auction of the Leblanc property, and he prized them above anything that he owned. The Metropolitan Museum in turn bought them, still in their original frames, at the auction of Degas's estate.

Oil on canvas 47 × 36½"
Wolfe Fund, 1918
Catherine Lorillard Wolfe Collection

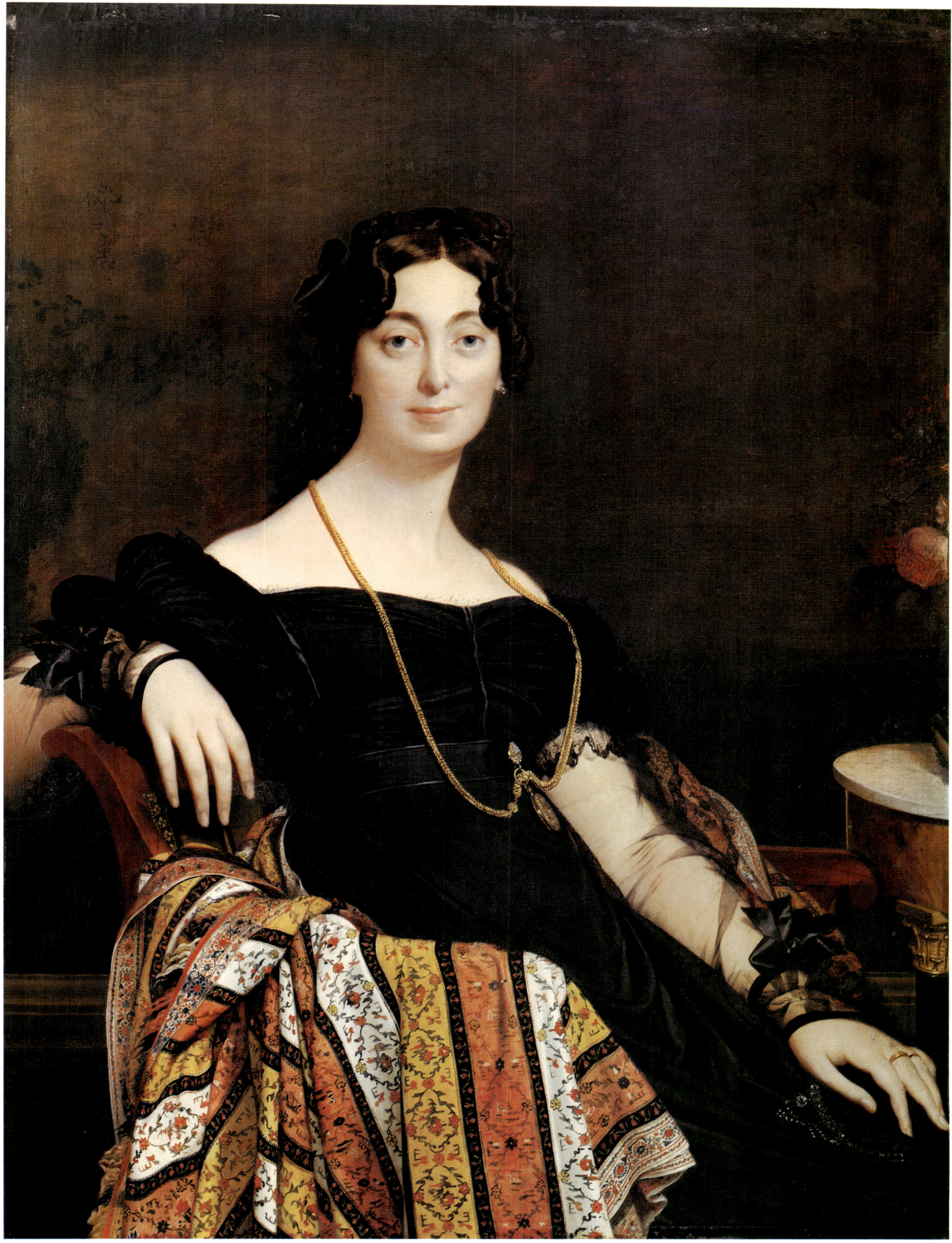

George Caleb Bingham, 1811–1879, *American*

FUR TRADERS DESCENDING THE MISSOURI (1845)

BINGHAM AND DAUMIER were almost contemporaries, and both recorded the life around them for a general public. Some of Bingham's figures, engraved on bank notes, were seen by as many people as Daumier's most popular lithographs. Both artists started at the bottom with ill-paid chores and pulled themselves up by their mostly unaided efforts. Bingham received enough encouragement from Chester Harding (then painting portraits in Missouri) to spend three months at the Pennsylvania Academy when he was thirty. Then in New York he found his subject matter by seeing W.S. Mount's success with genre paintings.

During his career he sold about twenty paintings to the American Art Union, which paid seventy-five dollars for this eerie vision of fur traders drifting in a dugout canoe down the wide Missouri to sell their pelts in New Orleans. The Art Union tactfully modified the artist's original title "French Trader and his Half-breed Son." For about ten years from 1839 until a lottery law stopped it, the Art Union distributed works of art to a wider, more democratic public than any American agency ever by appealing both to sound investors and to gamblers. Subscribers were sure of receiving an annual engraving of a well-chosen painting (often by Bingham), while a Christmas lottery surprised a lucky few with a marble Venus or a real oil painting. In this way our fur traders landed in Alabama.

Oil on canvas 29 × 36½"
Morris K. Jessup Fund, 1933

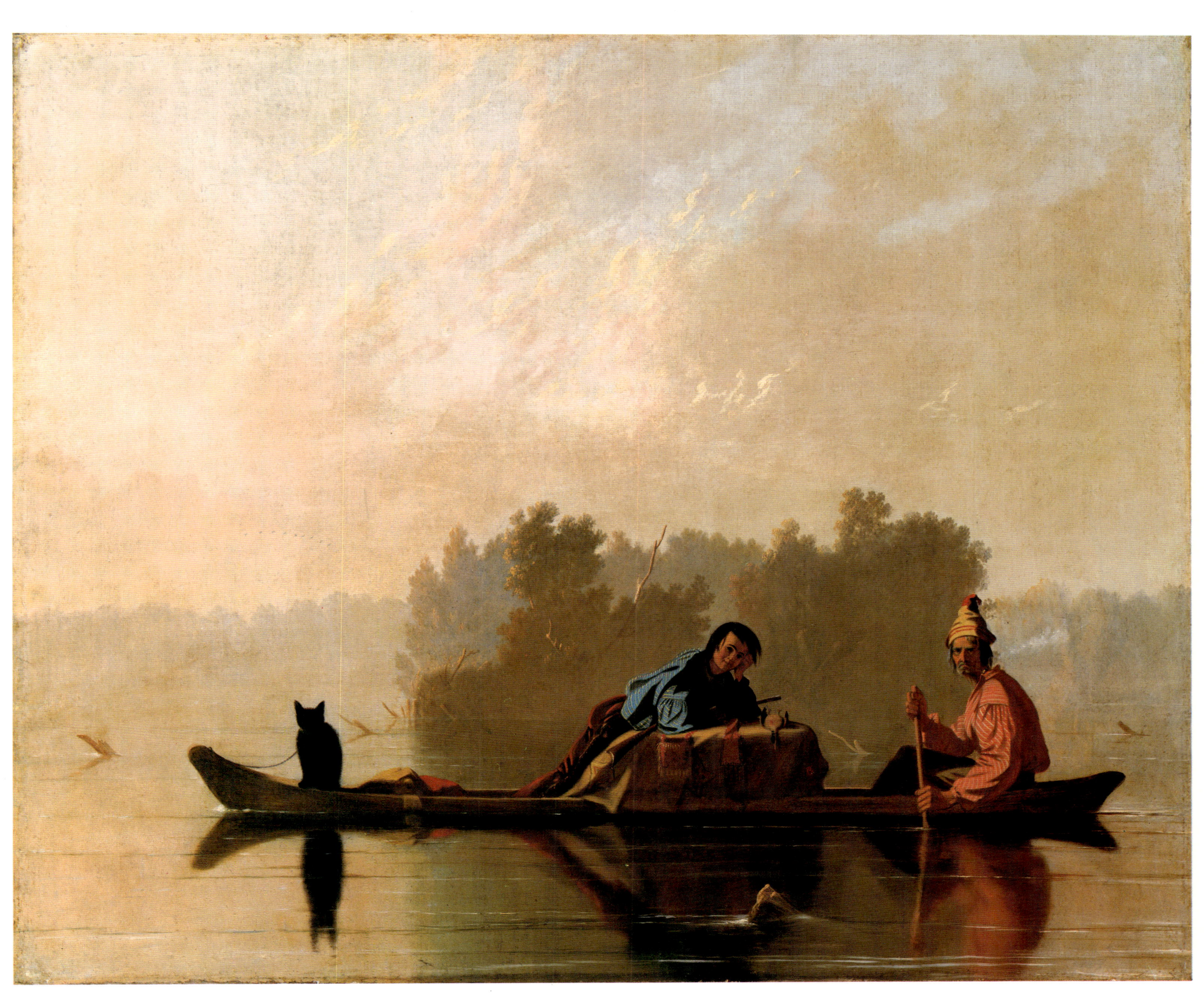

Honoré Daumier, 1808–1879, *French*

THE THIRD-CLASS CARRIAGE

IN HIS BOYHOOD DAUMIER helped to support his family by running errands in their poor quarter of Paris, where cheap rents attracted the first struggling lithographic presses. These presses took his teenage drawings on stone. While earning a pittance with such potboilers, he studied Roman sculpture and Michelangelo's *Captives* in the Louvre until he was nearly twenty-four, when he began his life's work of supplying some three thousand lithographs to newspapers. All the while he longed to give his whole effort to what he considered the nobler art of painting. He got his chance when, at fifty-two, he was dismissed from his newspaper employment and tried in vain for three years to support himself by painting. Without a solid training in oil technique, he worked on his canvases the way he worked on his stones, by smudging areas of light and dark that he defined into shapes by drawing lines on top wherever surfaces bend sharply. With vivid directness he portrayed the life around him, enhancing it through an eye experienced in sculpture and Rubens. The heads in this painting might be Roman portrait busts traveling in the age when rails were stretching and joining in networks that transformed the world. If Daumier lived today he would be drawing us on airplanes, escalators, and subways.

Oil on canvas 25¾ × 35½″
Bequest of Mrs. H.O. Havemeyer, 1929
The H.O. Havemeyer Collection

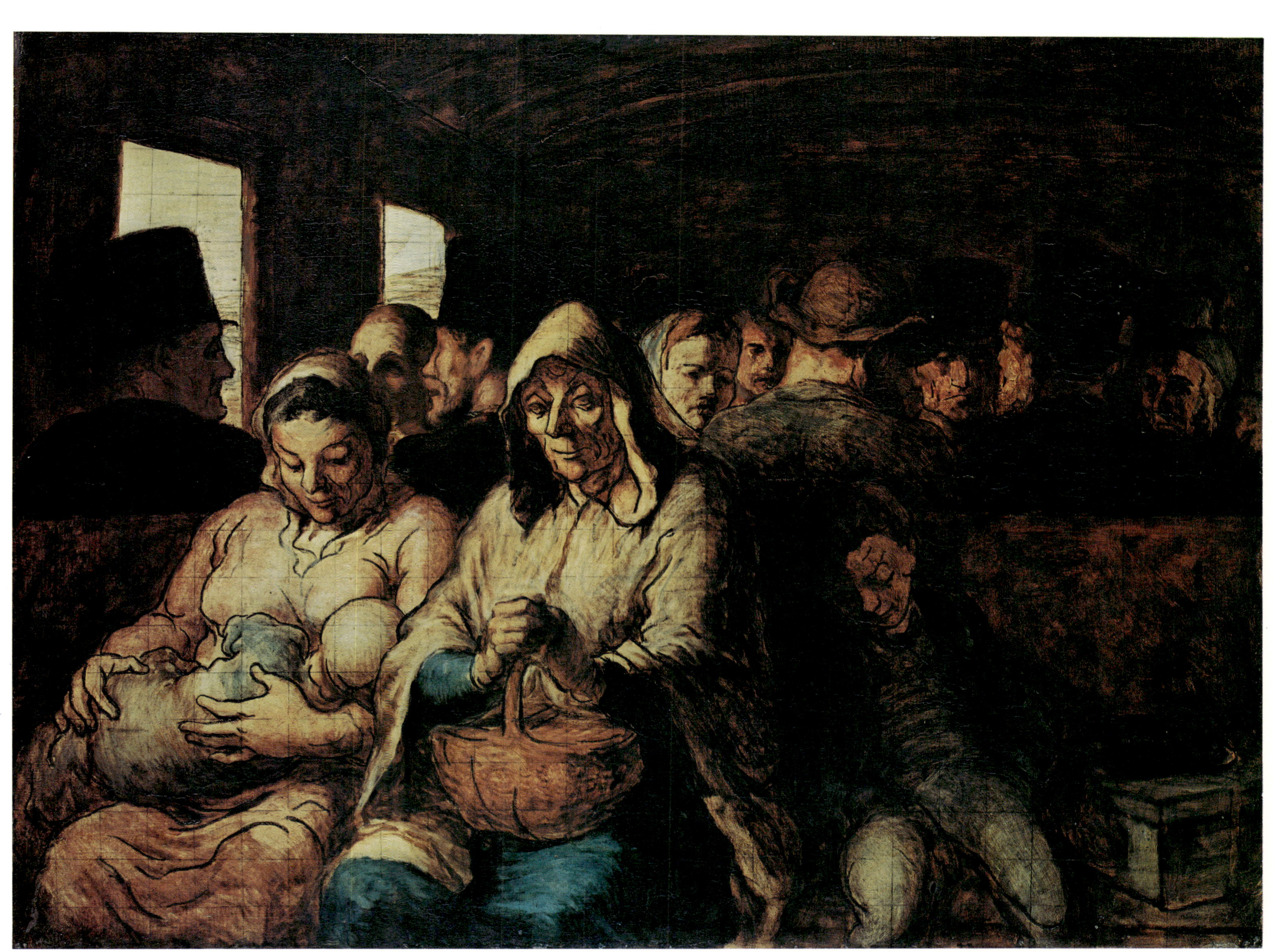

Édouard Manet, 1832–1883, *French*

WOMAN WITH A PARROT (1866)

THIS PAINTING REPRESENTS VICTORINE MEURANT, who was not a professional model, but a woman whose distinctiveness in a crowd had attracted Manet in 1862. In his studio she dressed as a bullfighter for the painting in the Metropolitan Museum; posed for the *Railway Station*, now in Washington; and for the *Picnic on the Grass* and the *Olympia* in Paris. This picture was painted in 1866, just when the Empress Eugénie had abandoned crinolines and transformed women's silhouettes from balloon to column. In the Salon of 1866 the picture was widely abused, partly because the parrot reminded critics of Courbet's *Woman with a Parrot* (now also in this museum), which had caused a scandal in the Salon of 1865. Manet was blamed for putting no more emphasis on the face than on the lemon that was added as an afterthought for color. And indeed, Victorine looks quite different in each painting of her because Manet did not snipe at the secrets of character, like Degas, nor feel sensuously drawn to people, like Renoir. He rested his whole case on clear color harmonies and dashing brushwork.

Oil on canvas 72⅞ × 50⅝"
Gift of Erwin Davis, 1889

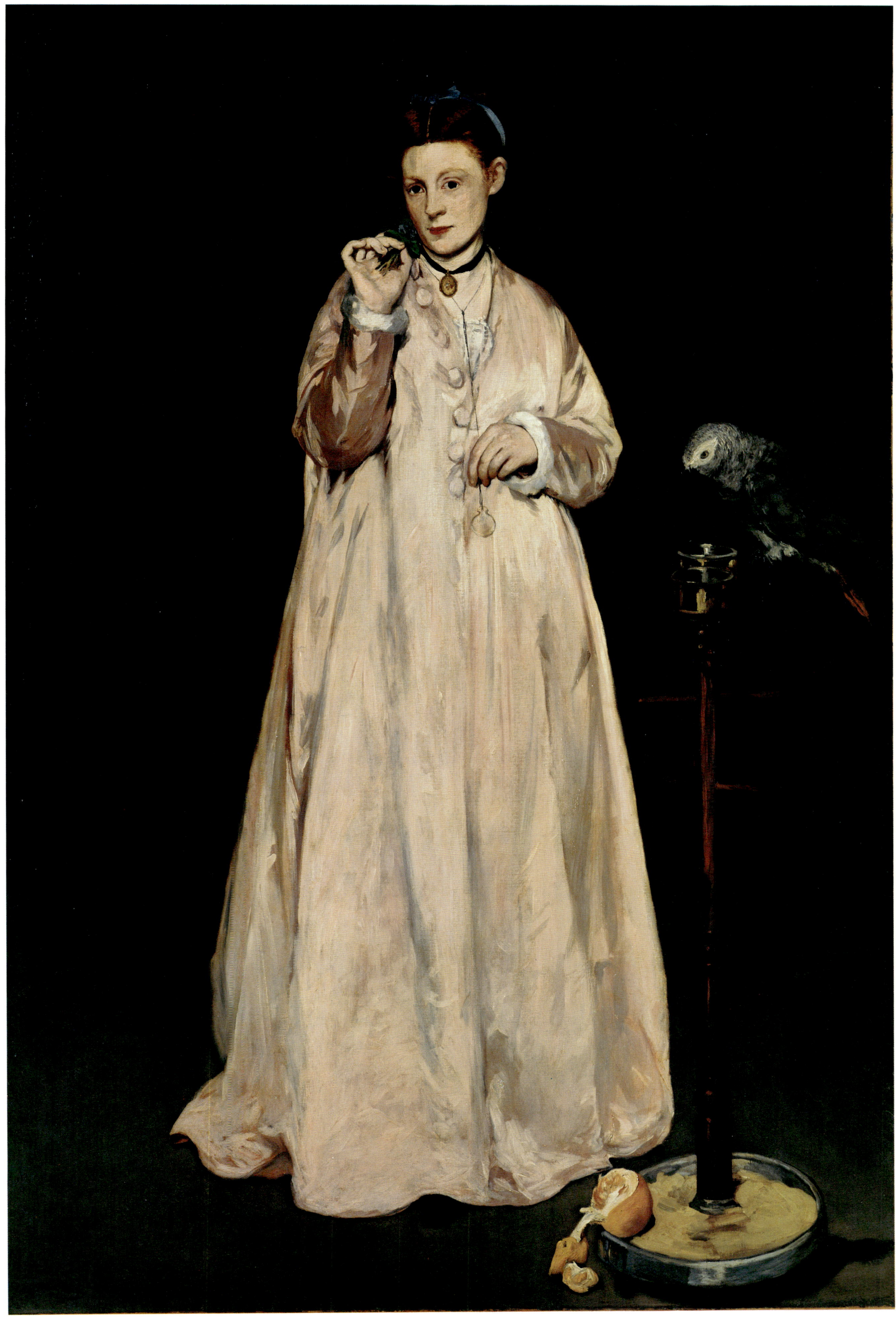

Martin Johnson Heade, 1819–1904, *American*

THE COMING STORM (1859)

IN HIS NATIVE BUCKS COUNTY, Pennsylvania, Heade was taught by his Quaker neighbor, Edward Hicks, the painter of *Peaceable Kingdoms*. He then set forth on discontented wanderings all the way from New York to Wisconsin, to the art centers of Europe, to Nicaragua, Colombia, and Brazil. At the last, when he was sixty-four, he married and settled in Saint Augustine, Florida, where Henry M. Flagler bought his paintings and gave him a studio in his new Ponce de Leon Hotel. Oddly enough, this visitor to the world's landscapes returned to very few subjects. He must have found a ready sale for dozens of banal little paintings of flowers, sometimes garnished with humming birds in jungle steam. In spite of his inland boyhood, he was inspired to his best work by the Massachusetts coast on the low shore of Narragansett Bay (the probable scene of this painting), and by the level Newburyport marshes, where conical hayricks acted like milestones measuring the depth to the horizon. As in the flats of Ruisdael's Holland, these New England lowlands lie like sediment under lofty skies of clouds, of sunsets, and of sudden summer storms. In painting these romantic transformations of light and weather, Heade had few equals.

Oil on canvas 28 × 44″
Erving Wolf Foundation
Gift of Mr. and Mrs. Erving Wolf, 1975

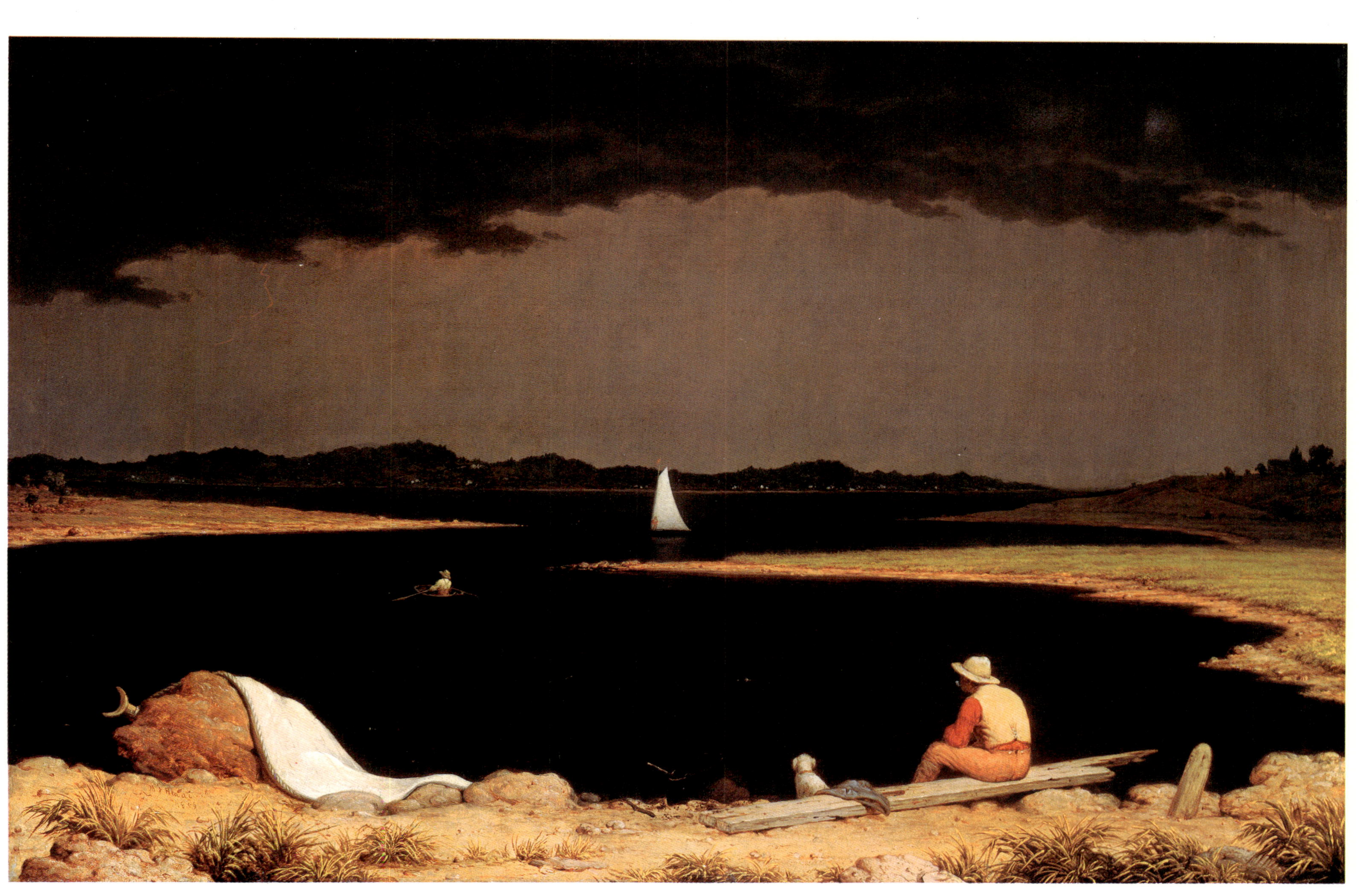

Thomas Eakins, 1844–1916, *American*

MAX SCHMITT IN A SINGLE SCULL (1871)

EAKINS PAINTED THIS PICTURE AS A PRESENT to his lifelong rowing companion. In the middle distance behind the professional champion who holds still as though we were photographing him, Eakins painted himself in the scull marked with his name. Eakins indulged his passion for geometry by working out the exact perspective of the iron bridges and even calculating the reflections in the ripples. The clear early fall afternoon is suspended in a magic of silence. Eakins painted this calm and startling picture a few months after returning from the strictest art school of Paris under the exacting tyranny of Bonnat and Gérôme. He was one of the first American painters to be polished by such discipline. As a result of this professional rigor, he was ignored as a stuffy Philadelphia academician. Time has brought out the originality of the unshrinking insight of his portraits and the lyric joy of his visions of action outdoors.

Oil on canvas 32¼ × 46¼"
Alfred N. Punnett Fund, and gift of George D. Pratt, 1934

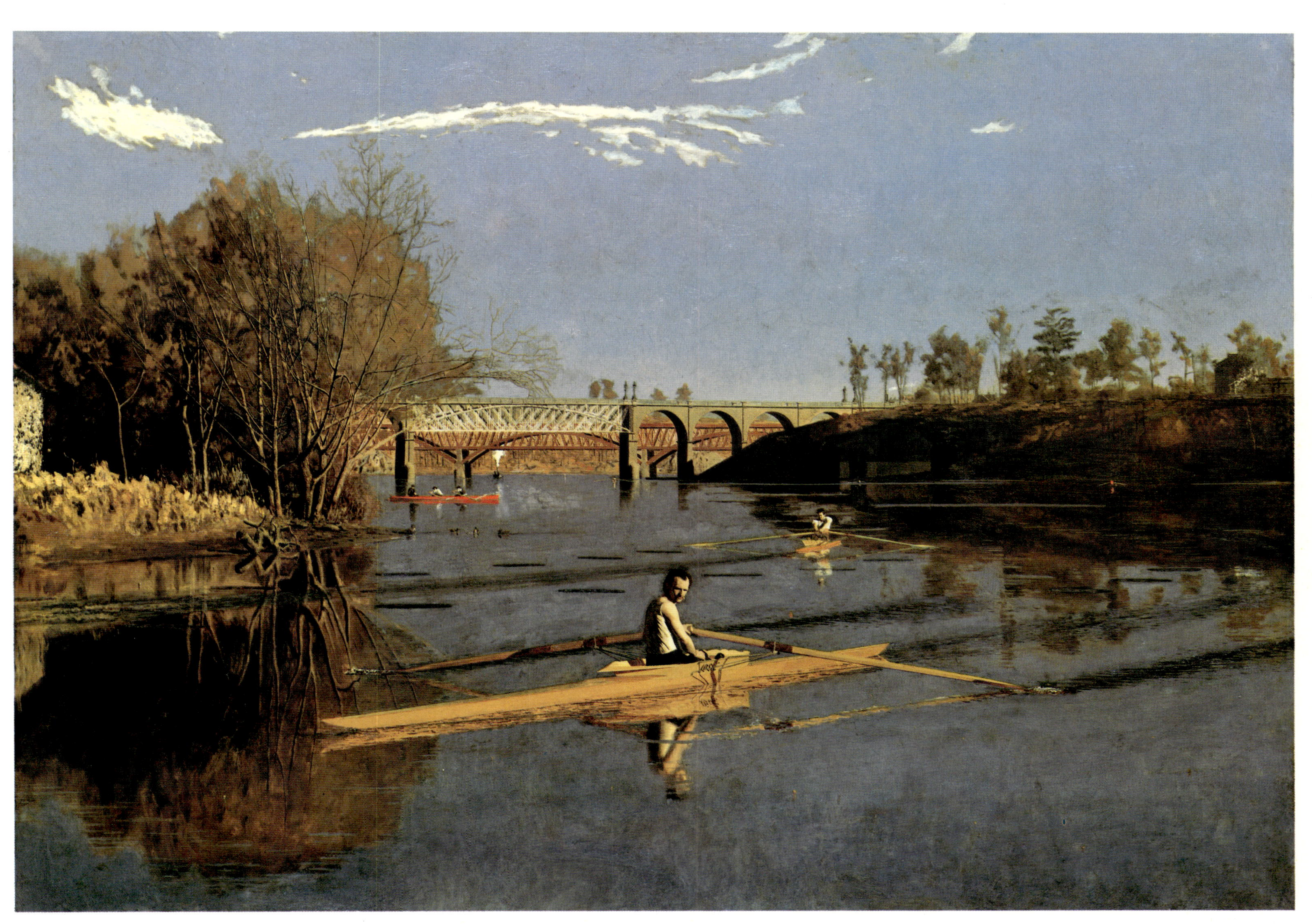

Winslow Homer, 1836–1910, *American*

SNAP THE WHIP (1872)

HOMER BEGAN BY DRAWING MUSIC COVERS and illustrations for books and magazines. This early start, and little instruction in oil painting, made his hand bolder on paper than on canvas. Another version of this painting was reproduced in a wood engraving in *Harper's Weekly* for September 20, 1873, toward the end of Homer's long series of illustrations of New England country life and of the Civil War, which he covered as its most vivid pictorial reporter. We today love his early works for idealizing American rural happiness without prettifying it, but they failed to charm some of his esthetic contemporaries. Henry James's word is bittersweet: "We frankly confess that we detest his subjects—his barren plank fences, his glaring, bold, blue skies, his big, dreary, vacant lots of meadows, his freckled, straight-haired Yankee urchins, his flat-breasted maidens, suggestive of a dish of rural doughnuts and pie . . . to reward his audacity he has incontestably succeeded." When the other version of *Snap the Whip* was shown in Paris in 1878, Frenchmen liked its novel freshness, but an English critic, his eye full of pre-Raphaelite exquisiteness, lambasted it: "What excuse can the painter offer for sending, and the judge and jury for accepting, under the head of Fine Art, such nondescripts as bear Mr. Homer's name?" Any such violent repugnance proves that an artist has broken the mold of custom with a new, raw-looking form. A work of art lives if it delights or enrages, but dies at a yawn.

Oil on canvas 12 × 20″
Gift of Christian A. Zabriskie, 1950

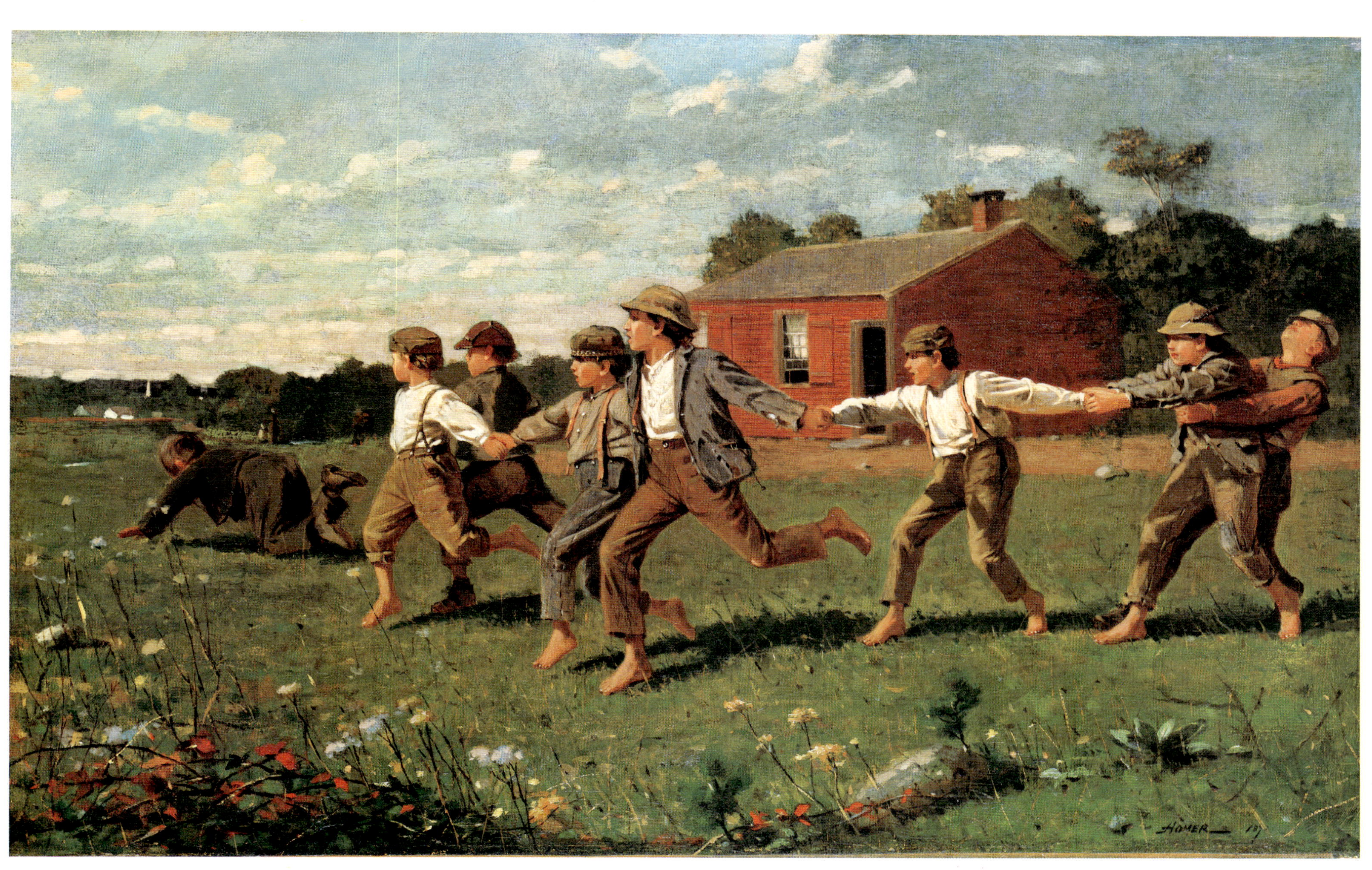
HOMER

Pierre-Auguste Renoir, 1841–1919, *French*

MADAME CHARPENTIER WITH HER CHILDREN, GEORGETTE AND PAUL (1878)

THE RUG OF A DOG—aptly named Porto—is suffering little children in the Parisian salon of Madame Georges Charpentier at 11 rue de Grenelle. There the slice-of-life writers—Zola, Flaubert, Daudet, Maupassant, and the Goncourts—met her husband, Georges Charpentier (1846–1905), who was the publisher of their novels and plays. His brilliant career was shattered in 1895 by the death of his twenty-year-old son Paul, here sitting beside his mother in girl's clothes because he is under five years old. This impending tragedy lends poignancy to one of the most poetic of all family portraits. Proust said that this portrait summed up the charm of family life in France during the nineteenth century. Because of the importance of the Charpentiers, Renoir composed this picture with an unusual care that makes it one of his two or three greatest achievements. He was right, for its acclaim in the Salon of 1879 opened his road to success.

Oil on canvas 60½ × 74⅛"
Wolfe Fund, 1907
Catherine Lorillard Wolfe Collection

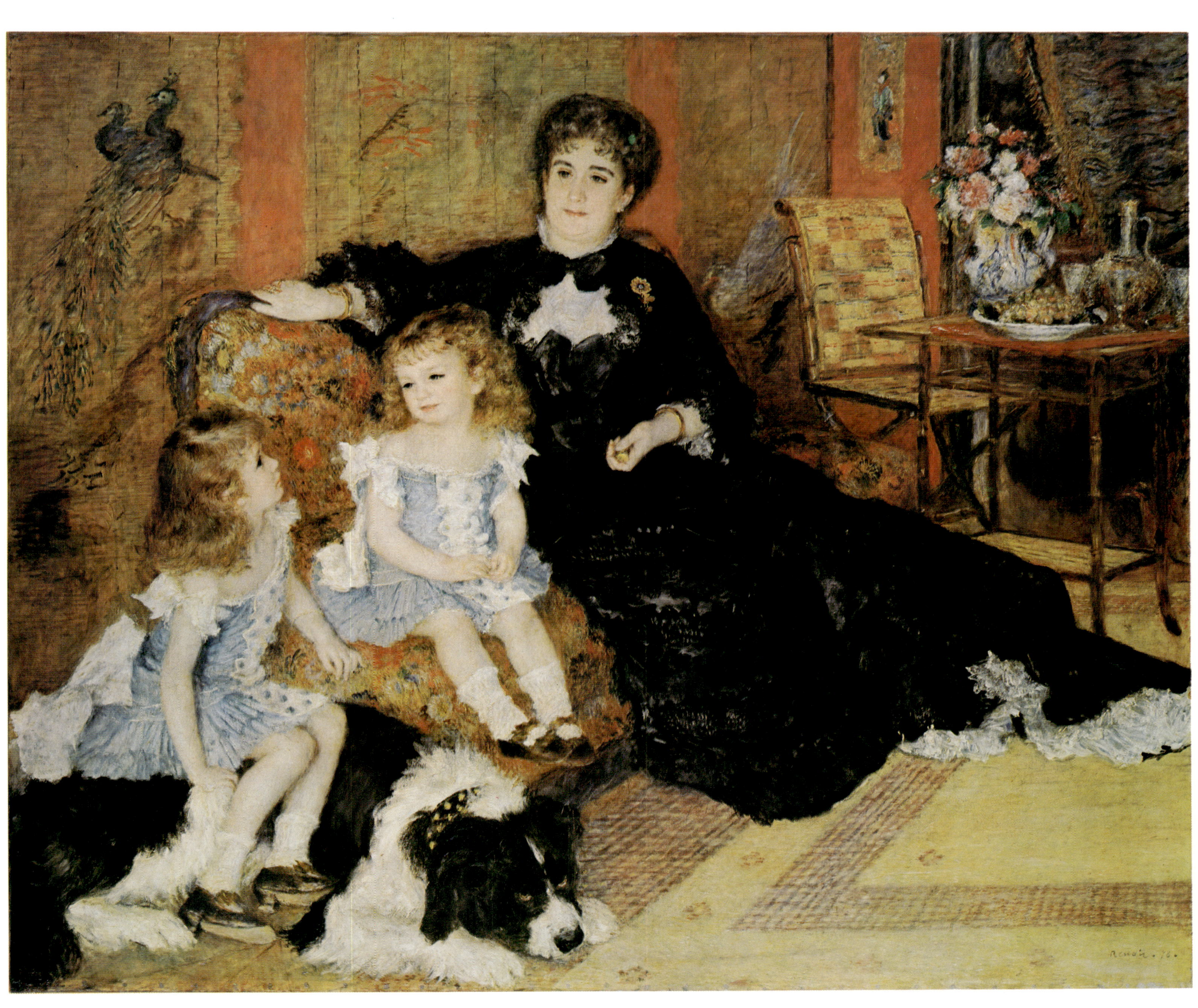
Renoir

Hilaire-Germain-Edgar Degas, 1834–1917, *French*

AT THE MILLINER'S (1882)

DEGAS, LIKE DAUMIER, searched for subjects where no painter had found them before. He then gave distinction to commonplace scenes by sneaking up on them from an unexpected angle, for he said that a painting requires as much stealth, as much plotting as a murder. This picture is sliced and divided like a Japanese print where people adapt to an imposed geometry of post and lattice. Mary Cassatt is said to have posed for the lady who is trying on the hat with the noble grace of an antique dryad listening to a Homeric echo. Degas's pictures fascinate by the passion and intelligence that had assimilated ancient and exotic works of art.

Pastel on paper 30 × 34″
Bequest of Mrs. H.O. Havemeyer, 1929
The H.O. Havemeyer Collection

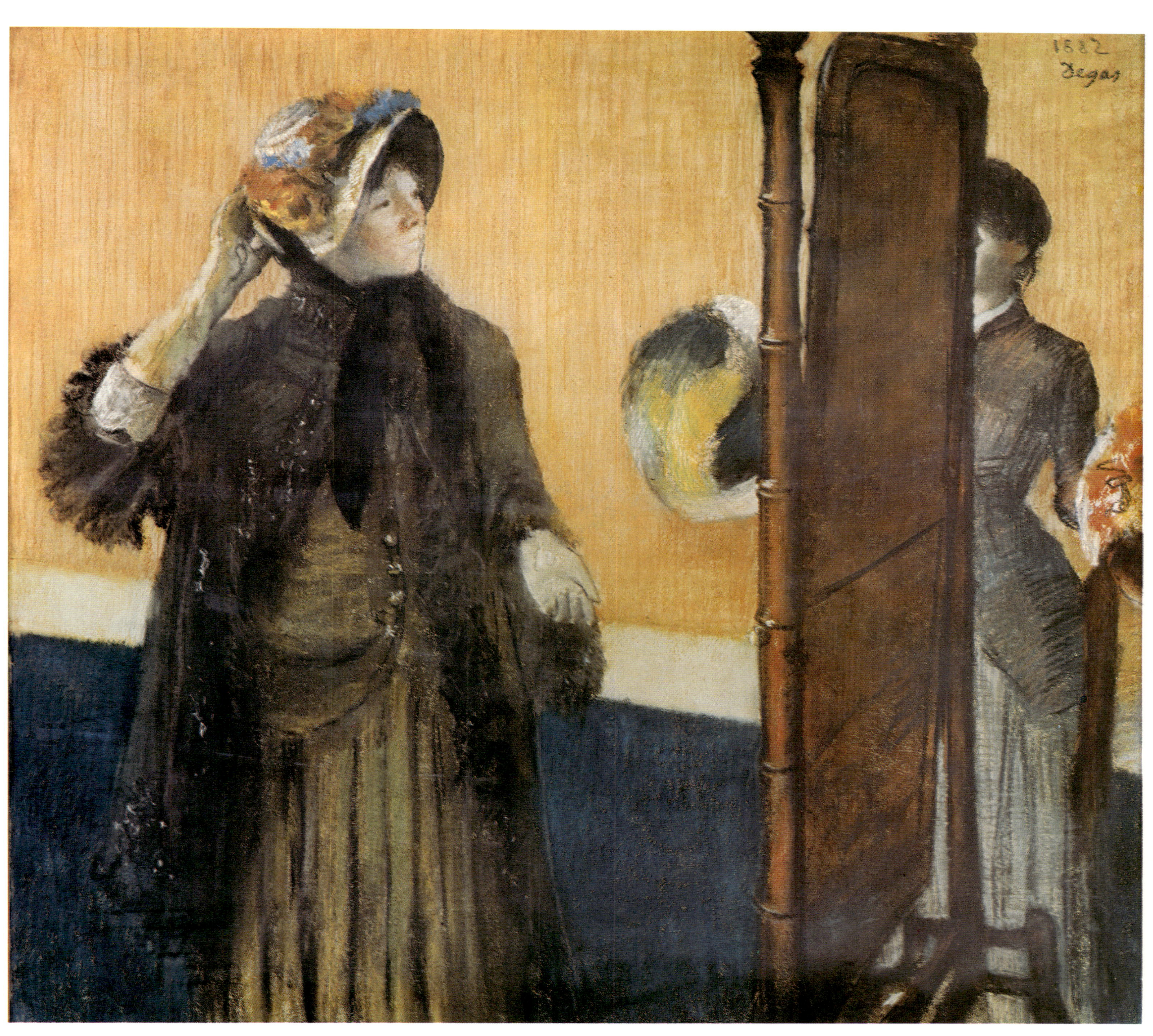
1882
Degas

Hilaire-Germain-Edgar Degas, 1834–1917, *French*

DANCERS, PINK AND GREEN (c. 1890)

In this late painting Degas's blurring eyesight eliminated details and saw colors in droplets of dazzle. He made oil paint glow like his pastels. He had also learned how to interlock the thrust and counterthrust of arms and bodies so as to wind up with an effect of perpetual motion. He said that you do not make a crowd with fifty people, but with five or six people. Since he was always fascinated by the professional gesture that reveals a lifetime of habit, he studied ballet dancers because they are formed, even deformed, by rigid calisthenics. It is odd that his pictures of ballet dancers should have exhausted the theme for other artists—the way Raphael exhausted the theme of the Madonna and Child—just when the Paris ballet had fossilized into a civil-service routine. Yet it is possible that the brilliant music hall personalities who sparked Toulouse-Lautrec would not have served Degas as well as his muddy little girls whose dullness offered no resistance to professional pressures. In a sonnet he said that queens are made of face paint and distance.

Oil on canvas $32\frac{3}{8} \times 29\frac{3}{4}''$
Bequest of Mrs. H.O. Havemeyer, 1929
The H.O. Havemeyer Collection

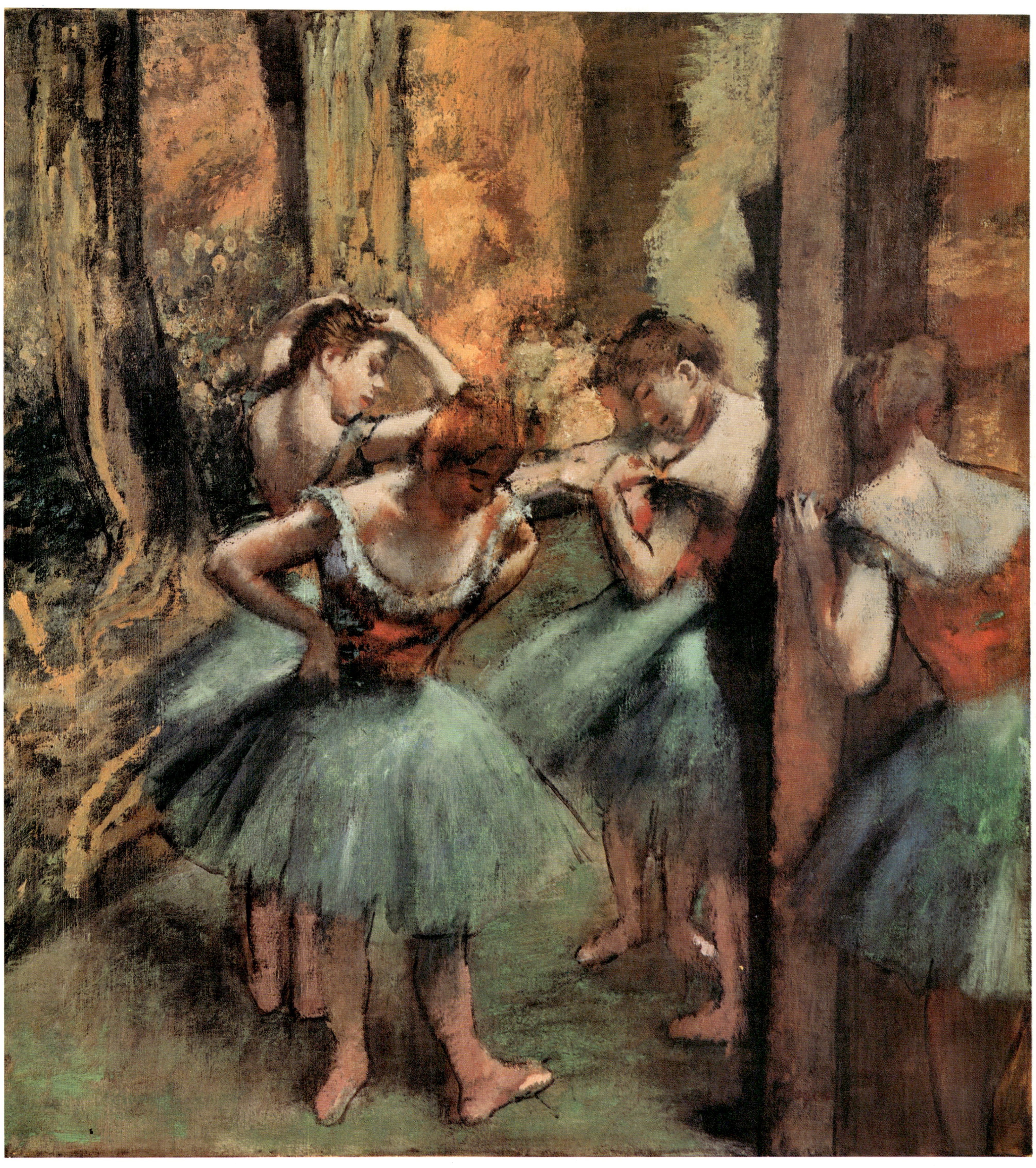

John Singer Sargent, 1856–1925, *American*

MADAME X (MADAME PIERRE GAUTREAU, NÉE VIRGINIE AVEGNO) (1883)

VIRGINIE AVEGNO WAS BORN OF French and Italian ancestry in Louisiana and married a Parisian banker in an age when a woman needed nothing but beauty to be famous. Her studied, indifferent, statuesque presence stopped parties, stopped traffic in the street. Ludwig II of Bavaria came all the way to Paris just to watch her, through diamond-studded opera glasses, as she made her slow way up the stairs of the Paris Opéra. Her celebrated profile and glowing hair challenged young Sargent to make many studies for this portrait during a summer at her house in Brittany, when she was twenty-four. In the Salon of 1884 the picture caused such an uproar that Sargent left Paris for London, taking the offensive portrait with him. Frank Jewett Mather analyzed the shock by saying, "The lovely body might as easily escape from its enveloping frock as a sword from its scabbard." But one day on the beach at Cannes, Madame Gautreau overheard a woman say that she was beginning to look worn. She drove in a closed carriage to her hotel, took a darkened compartment on the train to Paris, and shut herself up for the rest of her life in dim rooms without mirrors. For summer exercise she walked the beach by her country house, but only at midnight.

Oil on canvas $82\frac{1}{2} \times 43\frac{1}{4}$
Hearn Fund, 1916

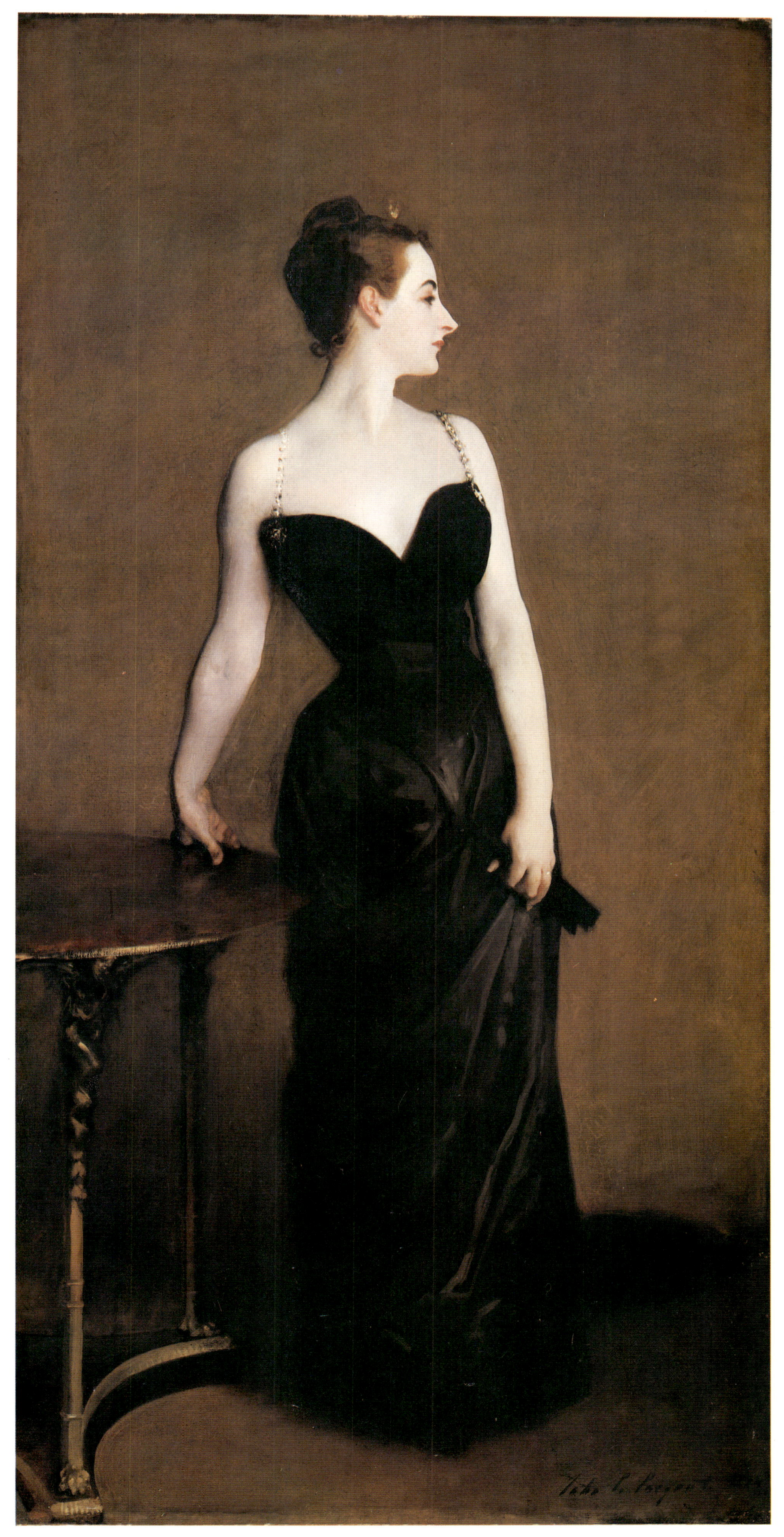

Paul Gauguin, 1848–1903, *French*

IA ORANA MARIA (1891)

BECAUSE *Ia Orana Maria* is Tahitian for "I Hail Thee, Mary"—the angel's salutation when he tells the Virgin that she will bear the Christ Child—this painting has been called an Annunciation in spite of the conspicuous boy Jesus. It is one of Gauguin's first works on arriving for the first time in Tahiti in 1891. He saw the natives there as he had seen the peasants in Brittany, through preconceived ideas of what primitive peoples should be. The two worshippers standing in the background of this picture, for instance, are adapted from a photograph of a stone relief in the ninth-century Javanese temple of Boro-Budur. When Gauguin's partly literary bias could work all alone with the bright colors, the tropical sun, and the indolent, bland Polynesians, he was free to invent a never-never land of voluptuous decoration.

Oil on canvas 44¾ × 34½"
Bequest of Sam A. Lewisohn, 1951

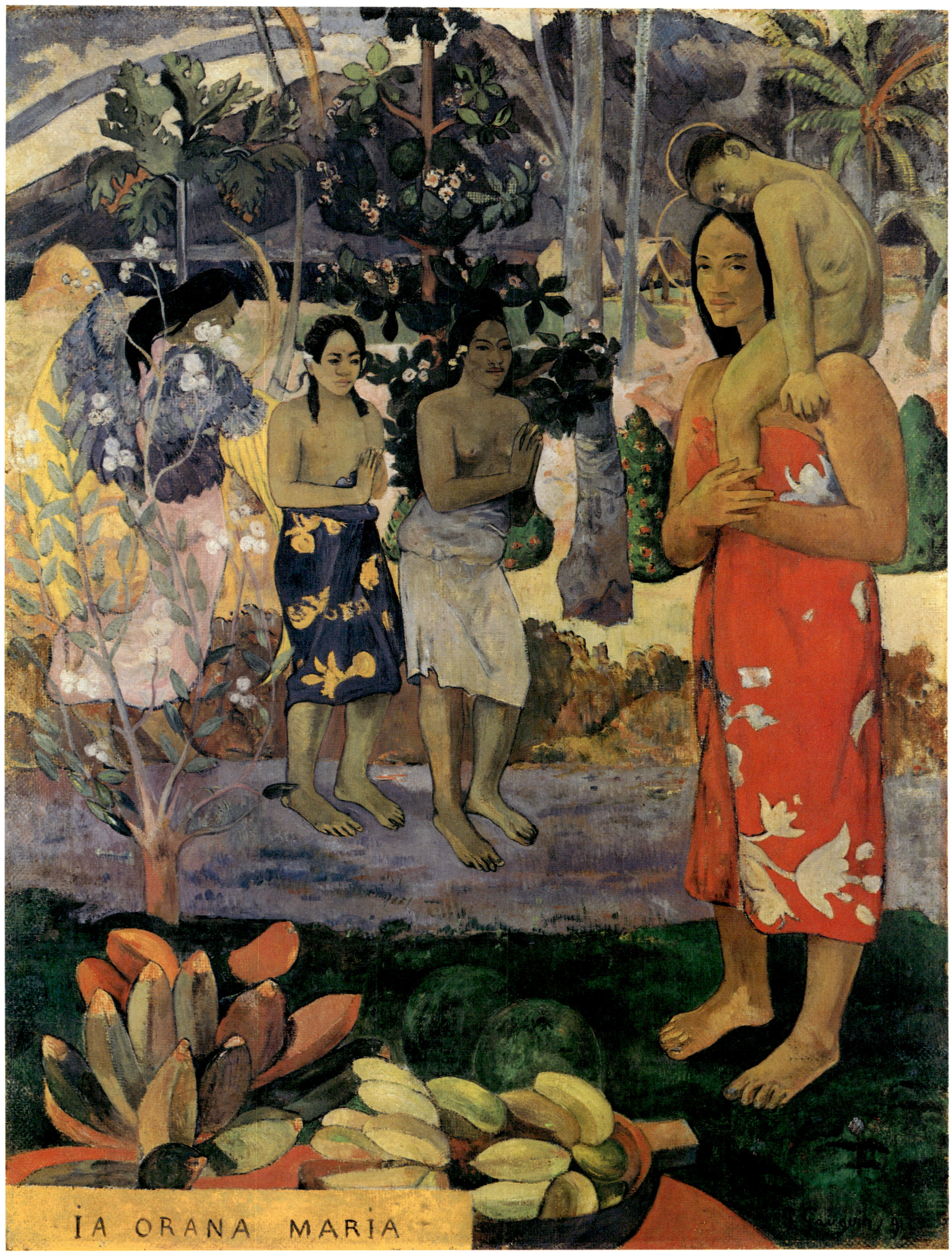
IA ORANA MARIA

Albert Pinkham Ryder, 1847–1917, *American*

MOONLIGHT MARINE (1870s–1880s)

A BOYHOOD ON THE BEACHES OF New Bedford started the sea surging through Ryder's dreams for the rest of his life. He practically taught himself to paint until he was twenty-three when he attended classes at the National Academy. He then stayed on in New York, living like a hermit and often walking the streets and parks all night to "soak in the moonlight." He reworked some of his small paintings for as long as twenty years, layering oil paint, wax, alcohol varnish, and candle grease in an interlarding that has fatally disintegrated the original deep jewels of color. He summed up his own work very consciously: "An artist should fear to become the slave of detail. He should strive to express his thought and not the surface of it. . . . He has only to remain true to his dream, and it will possess his work in such a manner that it will resemble the work of no other man."

Oil and possibly wax on wood 11 ½ × 12″
Samuel D. Lee Fund, 1934

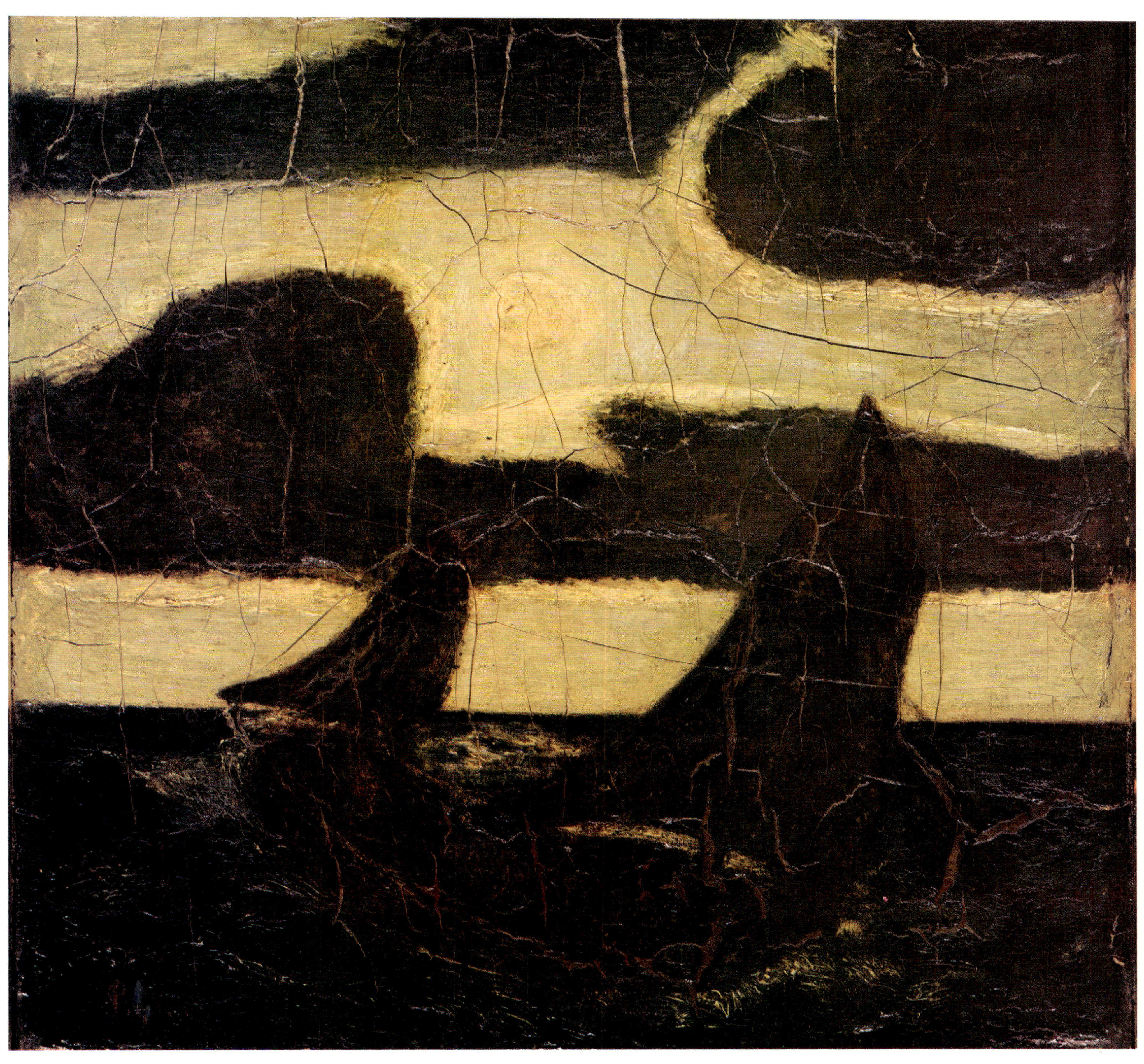

Claude Monet, 1840–1926, *French*

BRIDGE OVER A POOL OF WATER LILIES (1899)

MONET WANDERED ABOUT UNTIL he was forty-three, when he rented and later bought a house at Giverny near the Seine, to which he always returned after visits to Rouen, London, and Venice. He also bought and enlarged a pond near the river, planted it with water lilies, and built a bridge in a Japanese curve. In 1899 he repeated this view of the lily pond several times, lining up canvases so that he could work on one after another as the sunlight shifted. The lily pond inspired some of his greatest works when he sometimes painted the water as though it were simultaneously a surface at foot level and a mirror of clouds a mile down. This shifting ambiguity works its magic on canvases ample enough to prevent the eye from slipping off over the edge. It was said of Monet that he was nothing but an eye—but what an eye!

Oil on canvas 36½ × 29″
Bequest of Mrs. H. O. Havemeyer, 1929
The H. O. Havemeyer Collection

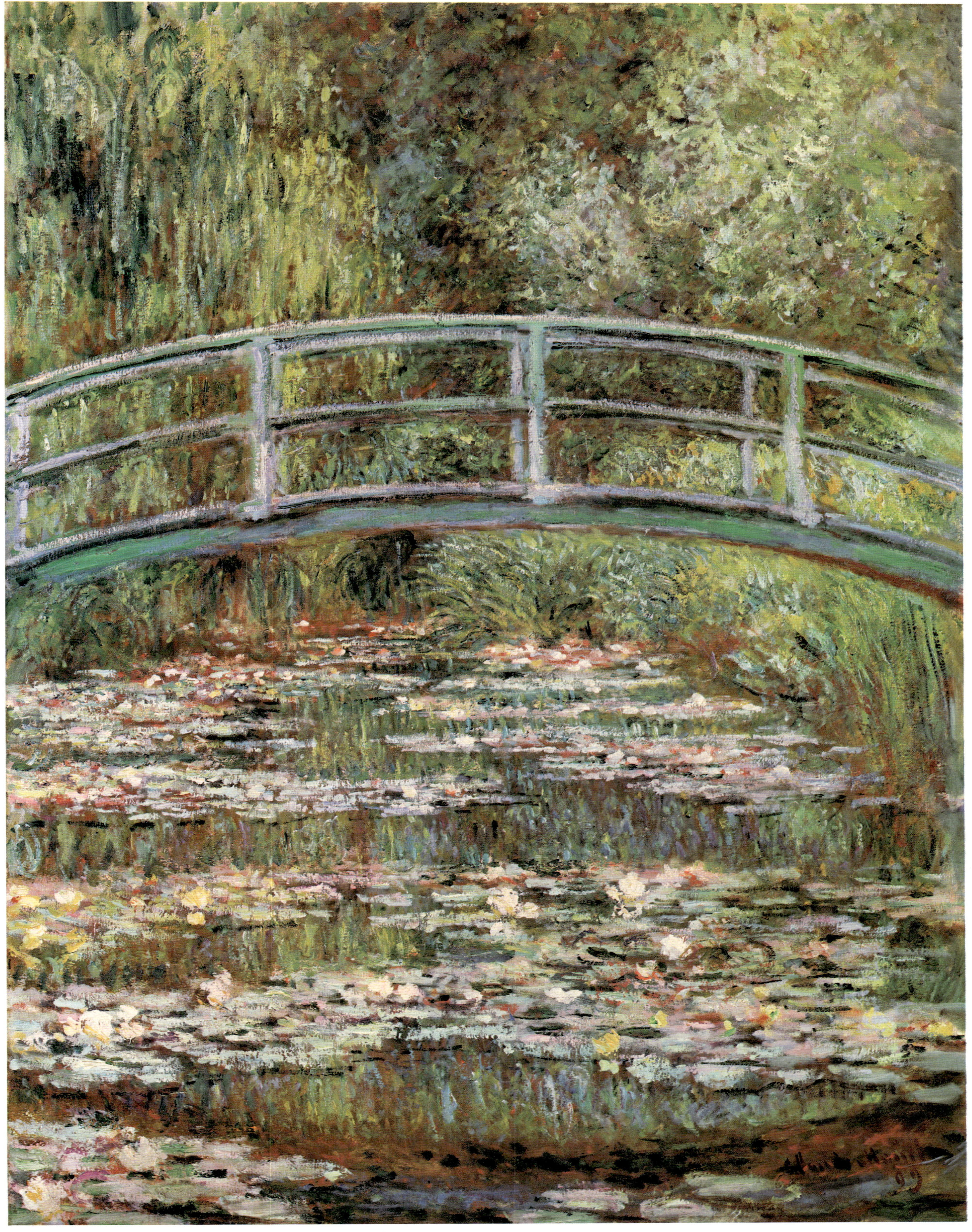

Vincent van Gogh, 1853–1890, *Dutch*

L'ARLÉSIENNE (1888)

VAN GOGH WROTE TO HIS BROTHER in November 1888 that he had "slashed out" this portrait in an hour. It represents Madame Ginoux, who ran the Café de la Gare in Arles, where van Gogh and Gauguin cajoled her into sitting for them by giving her coffee while Gauguin kept repeating: "Madame Ginoux, Madame Ginoux, some day your portrait will hang in the Louvre." This is the most spontaneous of five portraits that van Gogh painted of Madame Ginoux, the other four being from Gauguin's drawing, which van Gogh had with him in the asylum. The sunny flat background of this first version projects the sitter's snappy silhouette with the distinctness of a portrait by Pollaiuolo or Roger van der Weyden.

Oil on canvas 36 × 29″
Bequest of Sam A. Lewisohn, 1951

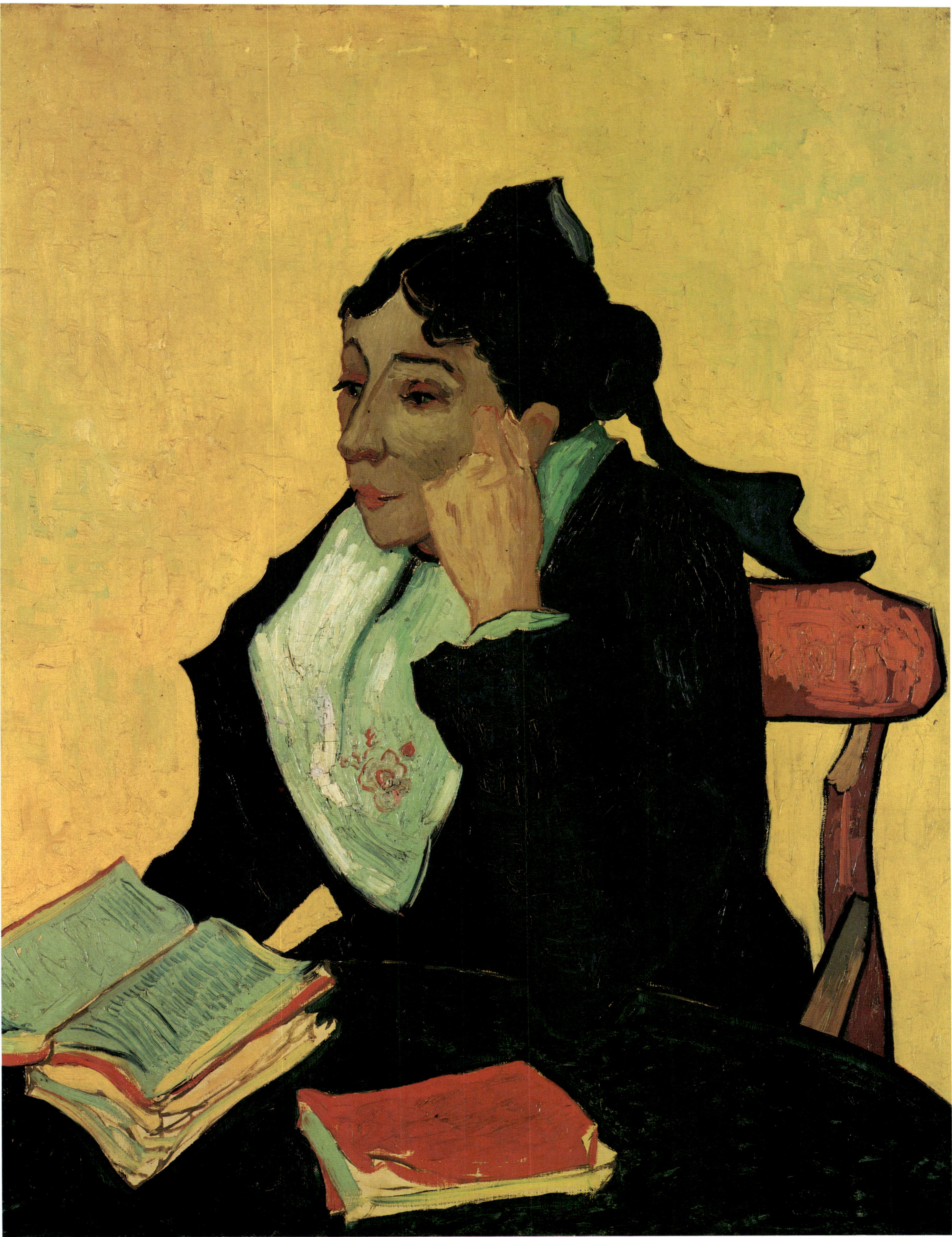

Henri-Marie-Raymond de Toulouse-Lautrec Monfa,

1864–1901, *French*

THE ENGLISHMAN AT THE MOULIN ROUGE (1892)

THIS IS A STUDY FOR Lautrec's second Moulin Rouge poster. The first, for the opening of the Moulin Rouge in October 1889, helped it to attract adventurers from the underworld all the way up to the Prince de Sagan, Prince Troubetskoy, the Duc de Talleyrand, Arthur Symonds, Oscar Wilde, and the Prince of Wales. In the crowd Lautrec was struck by the smartly dressed assurance of a young Englishman, William Tom Warrener (1861–1934), who had been exhibiting his paintings in Paris for several years. He is here proposing plans to two cancan dancers in the famous dance hall. Warrener took this painting with him on his recall home to England, when he was about forty-five, to run the family coal business. In the fogs of the Midlands it must have reminded him of his nights of milling among the gang at the Moulin Rouge to the racket of the band and the thump of the dancers as they kicked the dust from the trembling floor boards up to the gas chandeliers.

Oil on cardboard 33¾ × 26″
Bequest of Miss Adelaide Milton de Groot (1876–1967), 1967

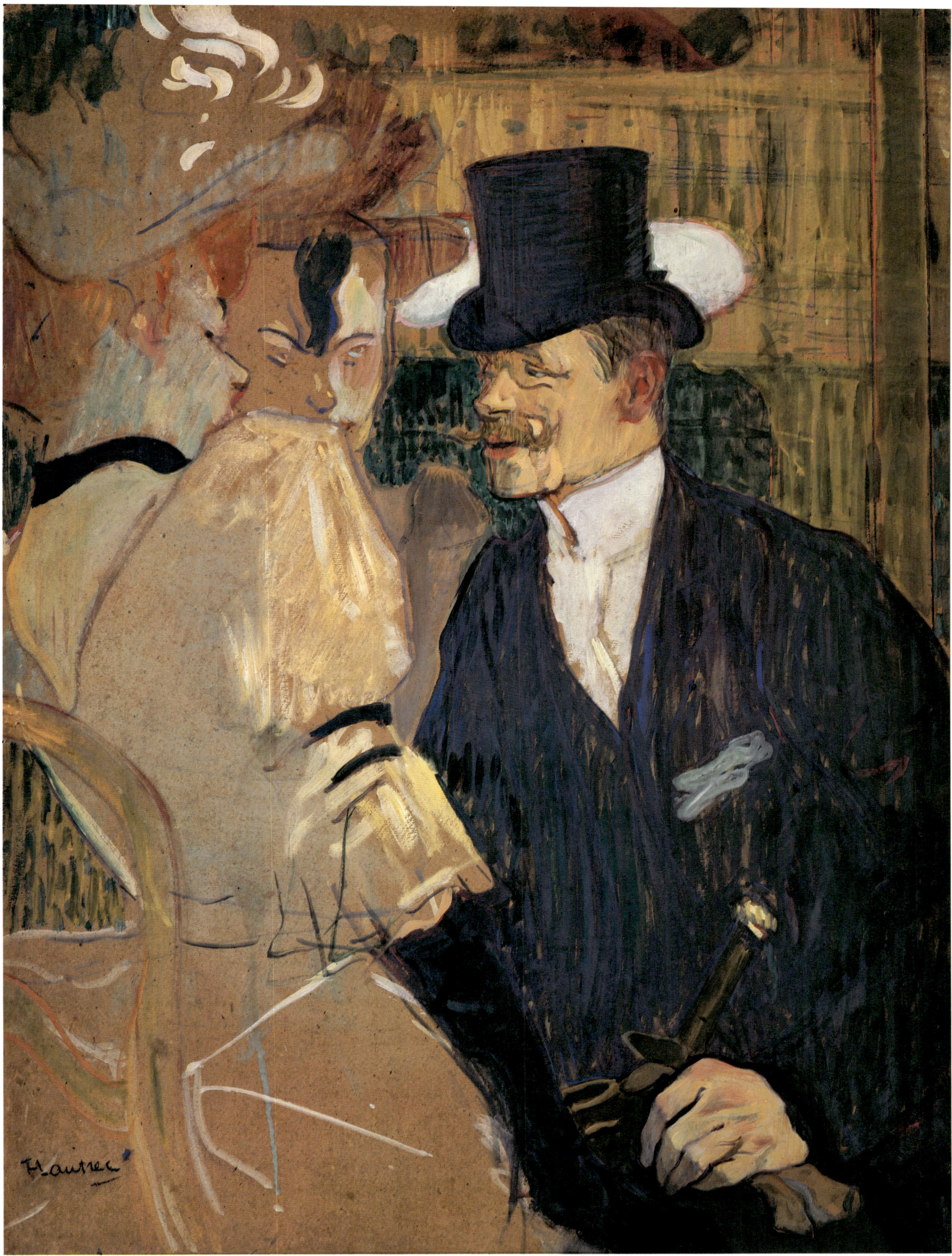
HLautrec

Pablo Ruiz y Picasso, 1881–1973, *Spanish*

GERTRUDE STEIN (1905–1906)

"PICASSO HAD NEVER HAD ANYBODY pose for him since he was sixteen years old. He was then twenty-four and Gertrude had never thought of having her portrait painted, and they do not know either of them how it came about. Anyway, it did, and she posed for this portrait ninety times. There was a large broken armchair where Gertrude Stein posed. There was a couch where everybody sat and slept. There was a little kitchen chair where Picasso sat to paint. There was a large easel and there were many canvases. She took her pose, Picasso sat very tight in his chair and very close to his canvas and on a very small palette, which was of a brown gray color, mixed some more brown gray and the painting began. All of a sudden one day Picasso painted out the whole head. I can't see you anymore when I look, he said irritably, and so the picture was left like that." (Gertrude Stein, *Autobiography of Alice B. Toklas*.)

Picasso got the resemblance in the massive hands and the slumped sandbag of a body. After he erased the face, he spent an interval during which he discovered primitive sculpture. He then came back to the faceless portrait without seeing his sitter, and imposed the intense, hieratic, discordant mask.

Oil on canvas $39\frac{3}{8} \times 32''$
Bequest of Gertrude Stein, 1947

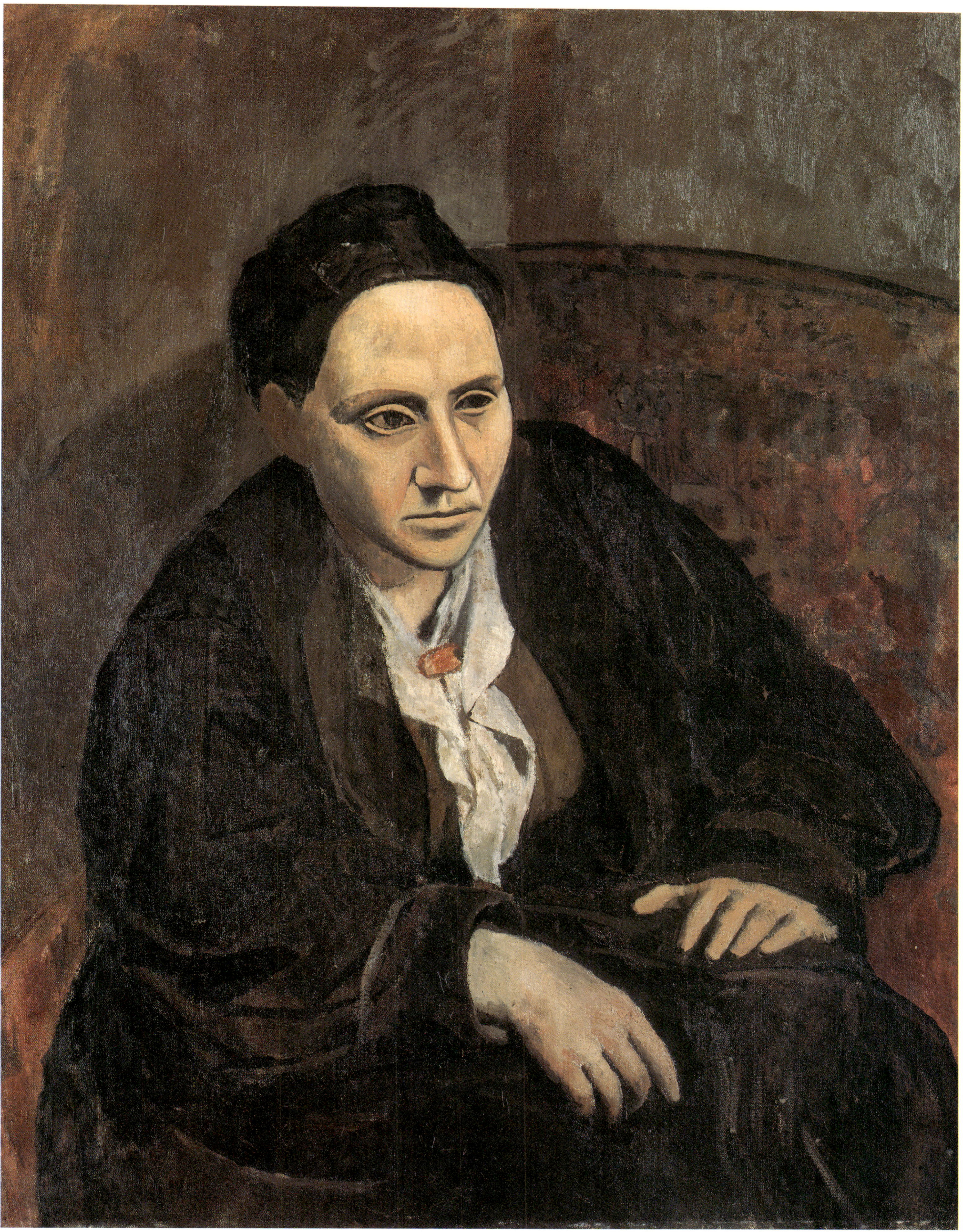

Amadeo Modigliani, 1884–1920, *Italian*

PORTRAIT OF A YOUNG GIRL (c. 1918)

After painting in Florence in the Italian equivalent of Impressionism, Modigliani went to Paris when he was twenty-two. There the discovery of African masks and idols started him chiseling wood and stone in sweeping planes. This sculptural geometry of curves did not kill his naturalism when he painted, but redirected it, producing portraits that vibrate with the strain of opposing forces. He managed to juggle his mannered line around the particularities of each sitter; his dinginess of mud and dust resulted in serenity and joy; his flat patterns conveyed the very breath of love. He seems to have painted this portrait in the south of France as he was dying of drink and tuberculosis. It probably represents Marie Feret, a peasant girl slaving as a household servant. Her uncomplaining submissiveness found an echo in Modigliani's devastating emotional discomfort.

Oil on canvas 23¾ × 18¼"
Gift of Charles F. Iklé, 1960

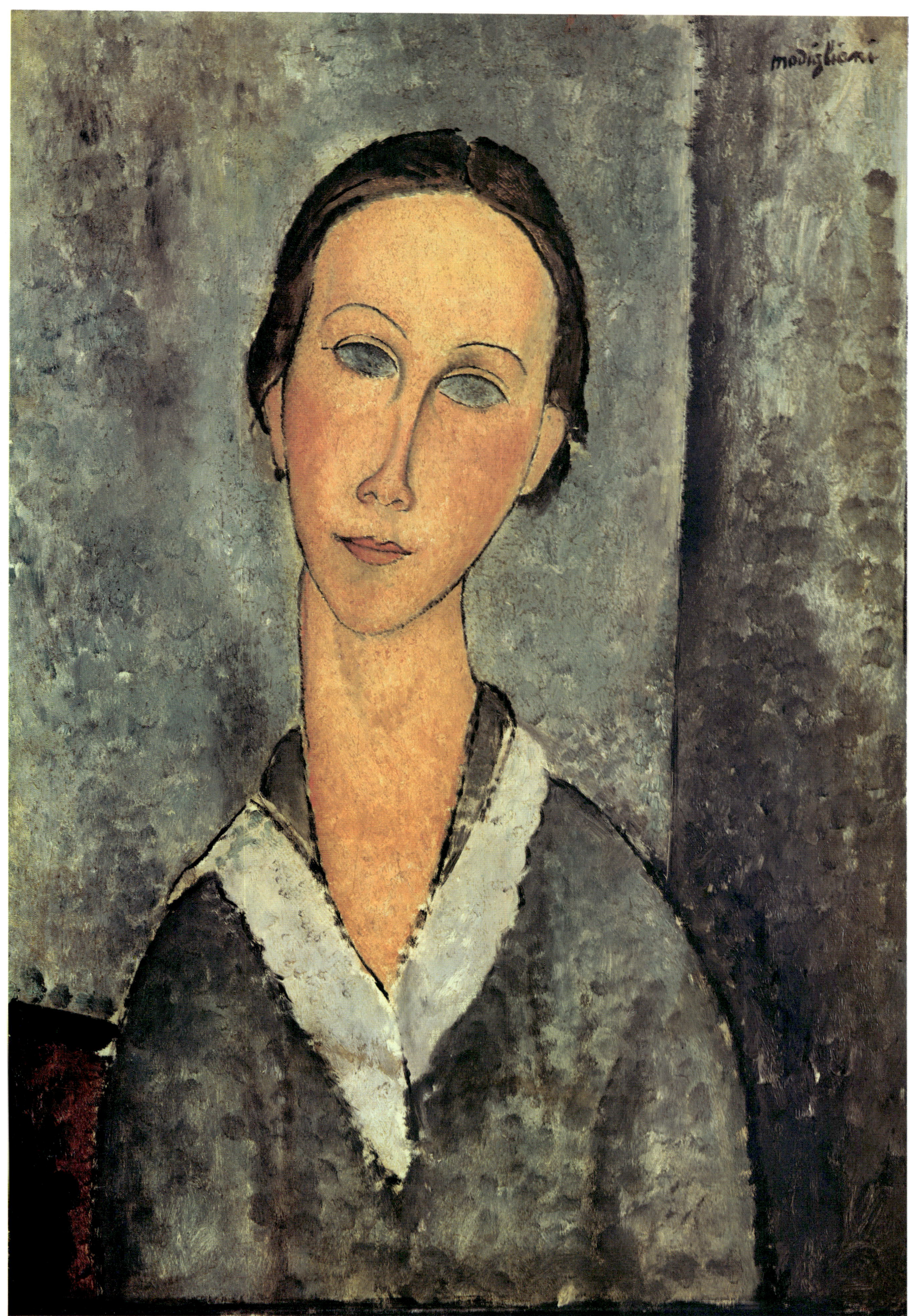
modigliani

Horace Pippin, 1888–1946, *American*

VICTORIAN INTERIOR (1946)

As a very small boy, Pippin could not resist illustrating his spelling exercises with little drawings of C A T, R A T, B O O K, even though this brought him scoldings and punishment. He continued to draw and then paint while supporting himself with menial jobs until he enlisted in the First World War. Then in France a sniper's bullet ended his active employment by paralyzing his right arm. Pippin used the leisure thus forced upon him to burn pictures in wood planks with a hot poker, supporting his right hand with his left fist. As he finished the burnt designs with paints, he became skillful enough to return to painting whole pictures. When he was forty-nine he showed some of his paintings at a shoemaker's window in his native West Chester, Pennsylvania, where they were discovered by N.C. Wyeth and Christian Brinton. This brought him recognition during his last nine years as one of the most gifted of our self-taught painters. He painted his black family and neighbors and the rooms of his house with direct truth and with the rich, dark sparkle of a born colorist. He spoke a truth that applied at least to himself when he said: "To me it seems impossible for one to teach another of art."

Oil on canvas 25¼ × 30
Hearn Fund, 1958

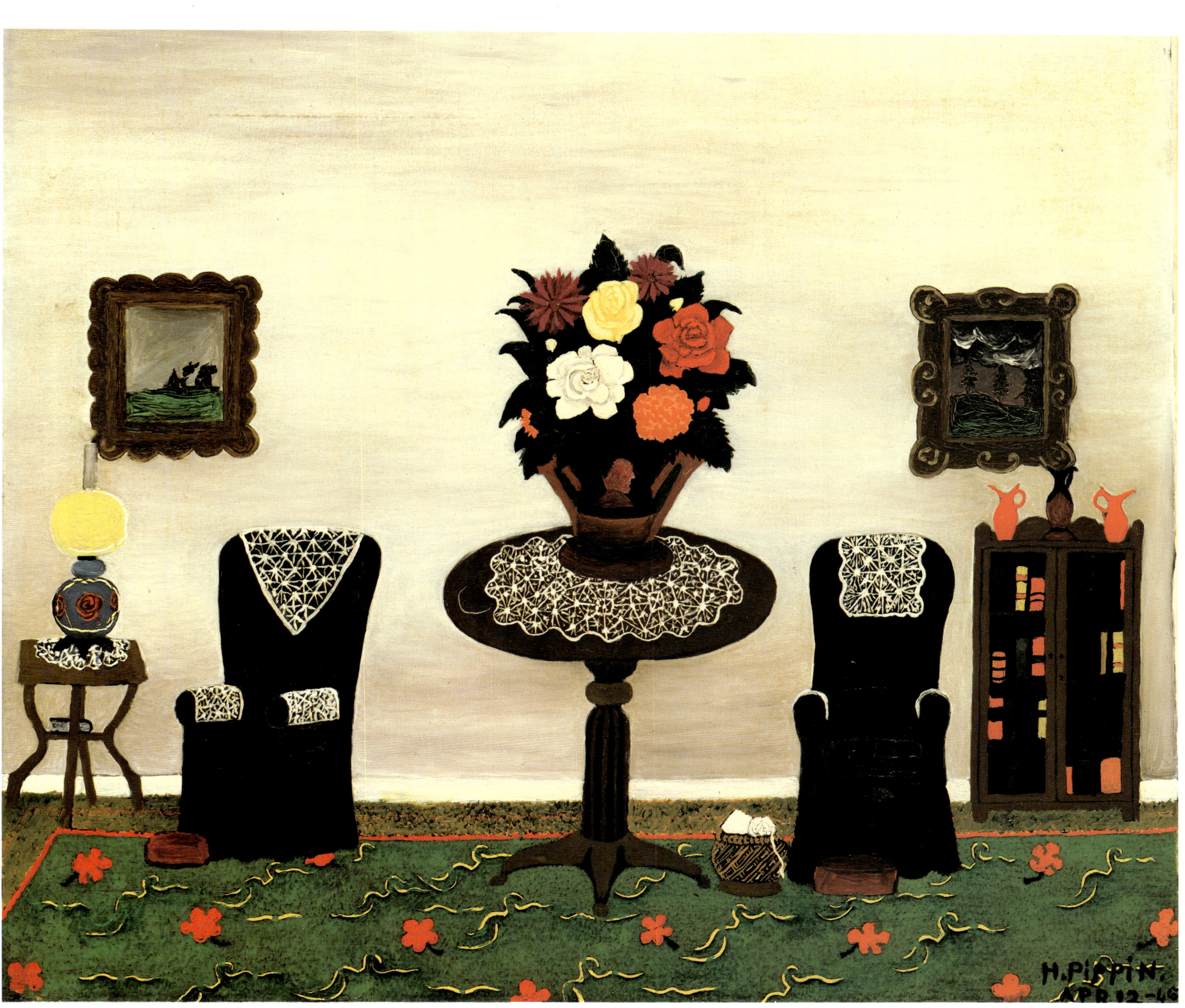
H.PiPPiN.
APR 12-46

Georgia O'Keeffe, born 1887, *American*

COW'S SKULL, RED, WHITE AND BLUE (1931)

O'KEEFFE'S PAINTINGS HAVE BECOME everybody's symbol for the great deserts of the Southwest, which she loves for "The openness. The dry landscape. The beauty of that wild world." She has clearly stated her aims in art by saying, "Filling space in a beautiful way, that is what painting means to me."

Oil on canvas 39⅞ × 35⅞"
Alfred Stieglitz Collection, 1952

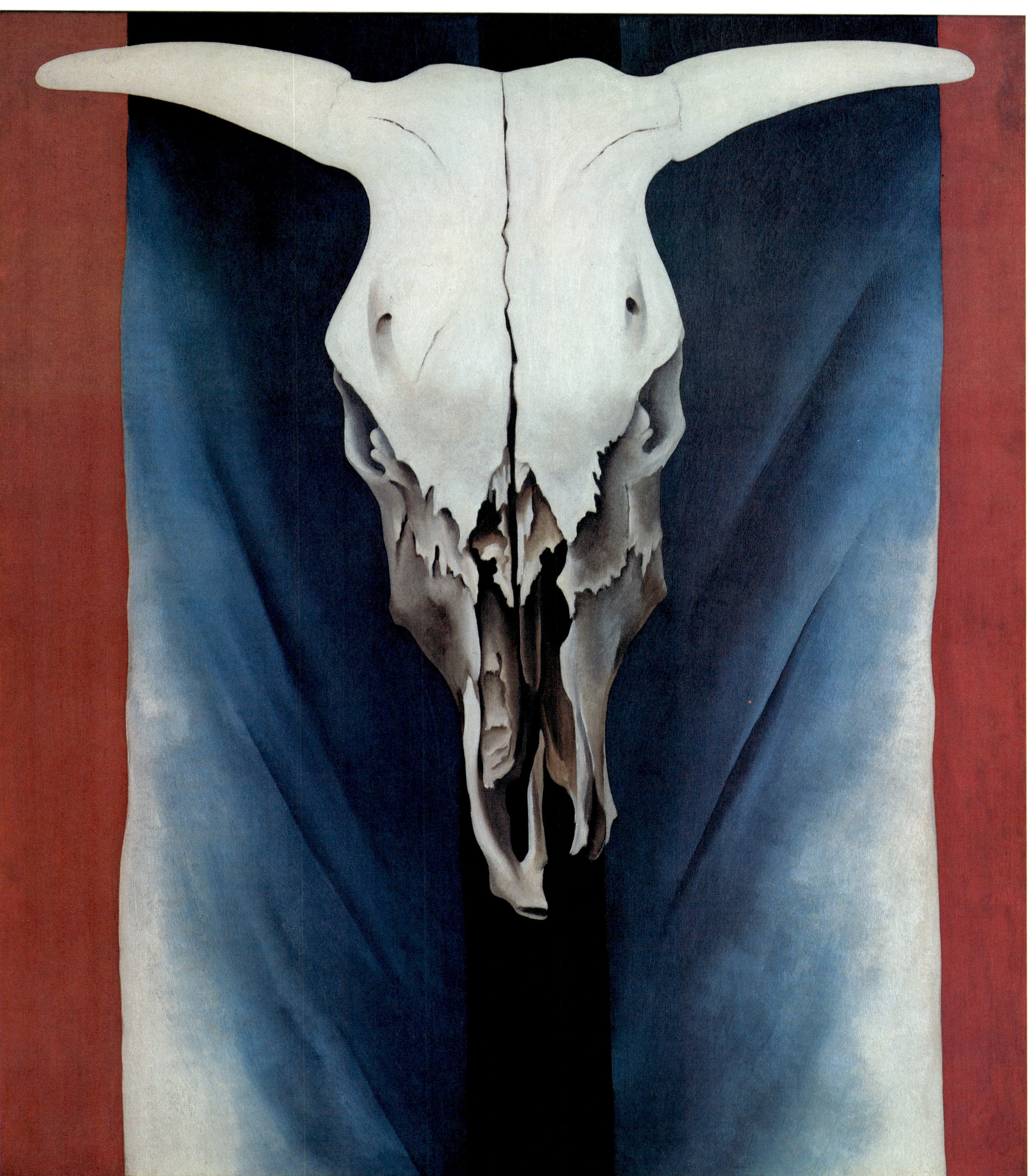

Charles Demuth, 1883–1935, *American*

I SAW THE FIGURE 5 IN GOLD (1928)

THE GREAT FIGURE

I saw the figure 5
in gold
on a red
fire truck
moving
tense
unheeded
to gong clangs
siren howls
and wheels rumbling
through the dark city.

This poem by the artist's friend, William Carlos Williams, inspired a painting that is not the usual literary illustration, but the vision of a parallel experience. The 5's run into the distance like the rush and thunder of the retreating fire engine. Their firm swing, clean color, and spiral springing showed the way, thirty years later, for Jasper Johns, Robert Indiana, and other painters. Demuth was equally sensitive in a quite different way when discovering visual equivalents in watercolors that mirror the moods of Zola's *L'Assommoir* and Henry James's *The Beast in the Jungle* and *The Turn of the Screw*. In his short life this quiet, very private man nudged American painting toward an unexpected direction.

Oil on composition board 35½ × 30"
Alfred Stieglitz Collection, 1949

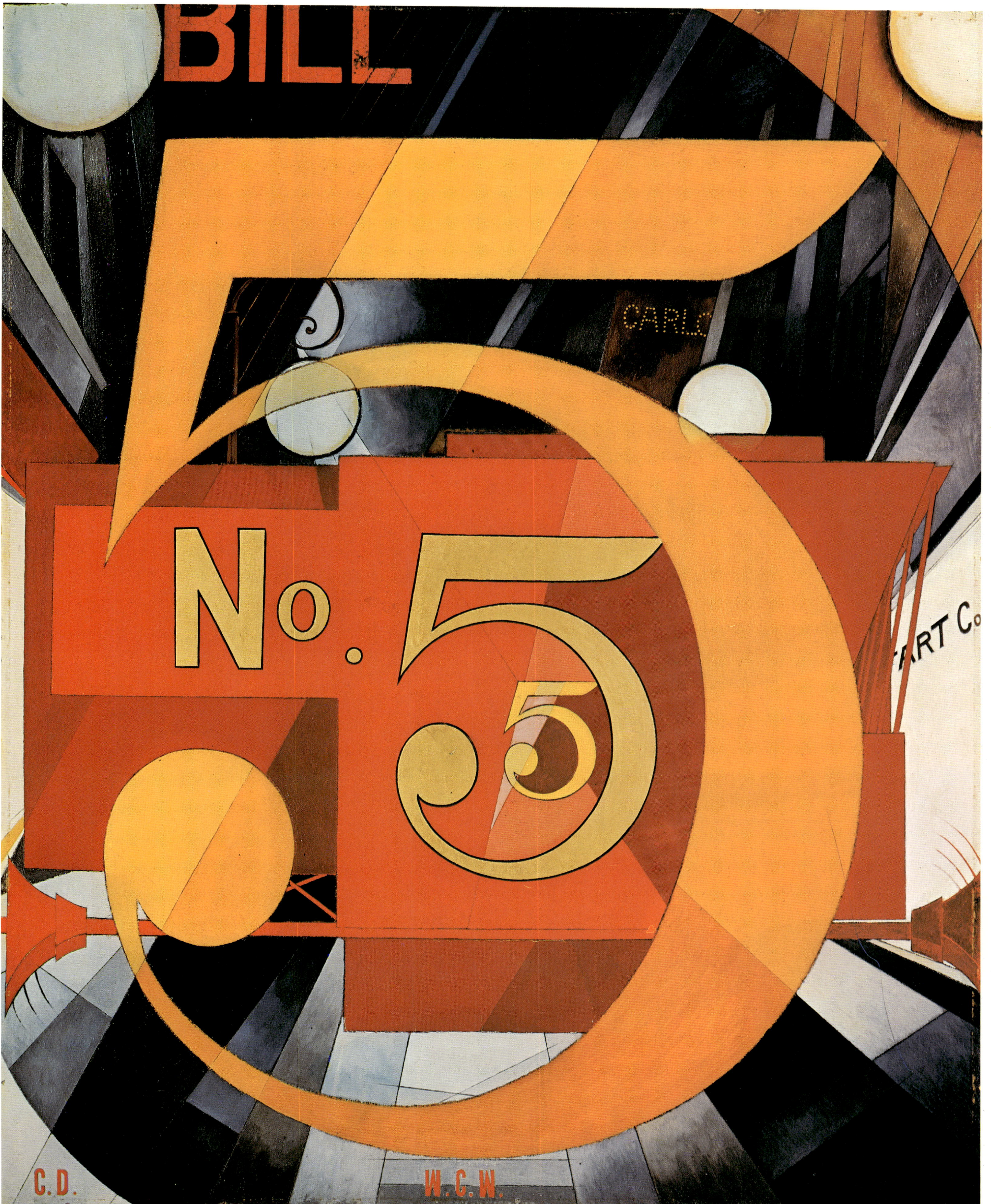
BILL
CARL
No. 5
5
ART Co
C.D.
W.C.W.

Charles Sheeler, 1883–1965, *American*

GOLDEN GATE (1955)

IN HIS EARLY TWENTIES at the Pennsylvania Academy, Charles Sheeler was trained by William Merritt Chase to catch the momentary shifts of sunlight. Then when he was twenty-five, Sheeler discovered Piero della Francesca in Italy, and Cézanne, Braque, and Picasso in Paris. The shock started him on a ten-year course of "bailing out" from Chase's improvising on glimpses. Sheeler put it this way: "One doesn't build a house just on impulse. They (Piero, Braque, etc.) didn't start piling up bricks hoping it would turn out to be a house. They really did have blueprints." When he was thirty-one he helped himself toward a vision of order through earning his living by taking photographs for architects. In 1927 his photographs became as important as his paintings when he exhibited thirty-two that he had taken at the Ford factory in River Rouge. By that time he was well on his way into the clean, precise painting by which he is remembered, and which he explained by saying: "Something seen keeps recurring in one's memory, with insistence, with increasing vividness. In the course of time the accumulation takes on a personal identity and the picture attains a mental existence." As his mind developed the germinating impression, the result sometimes superficially resembled abstract painting. He said that the title *Golden Gate* is "more fluid than if the bridge were added. Then it would be the connecting link between two dots on the map. It is an opening to whatever the spectator feels desirable."

Oil on canvas 25⅛ × 34⅞"
Hearn Fund, 1955

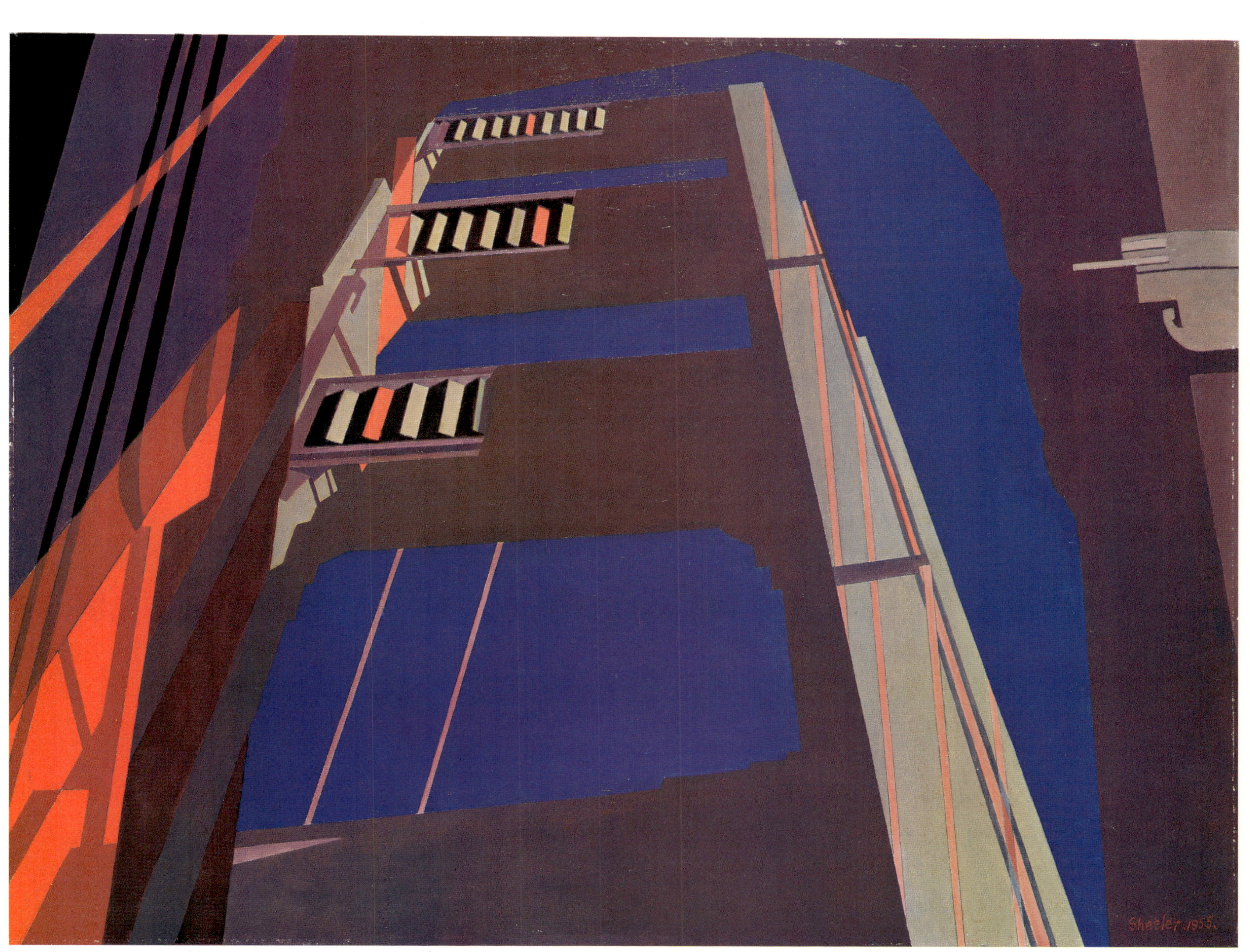
Sheeler 1955.

Edward Hopper, 1882–1967, *American*

FROM WILLIAMSBURG BRIDGE (1928)

HOPPER HAD TO LABOR IN NEGLECT until middle age before anybody noticed his work. His teachers, Robert Henri and Kenneth Hayes Miller, directed his attention toward the people he met in the city streets; but being a wordless hermit, Hopper looked past the people and saw only the streets. After selling his first painting in the Armory Show in 1913, he did not sell a second one for another ten years, when he was forty-one. While he supported himself by drawing advertisements and illustrations, he longed to "paint sunlight on the side of a house." Irksome as these commercial chores might have been, they exercised his handling of watercolor until he could start a serious painting with the difficult decisions of planning where to leave the paper blank. Long before the current interest in Victorian buildings, he resigned himself as an American to accepting "our native architecture with its hideous beauty, its fantastic roofs—pseudo-Gothic, French Mansard, Colonial, mongrel or what not—with eye-searing color or delicate harmonies of faded paint, shouldering each other along interminable streets that taper off into swamps or dump heaps." Hopper's paintings radiate a loneliness that expands right and left beyond the frame.

Oil on canvas 29 × 43"
Hearn Fund, 1937

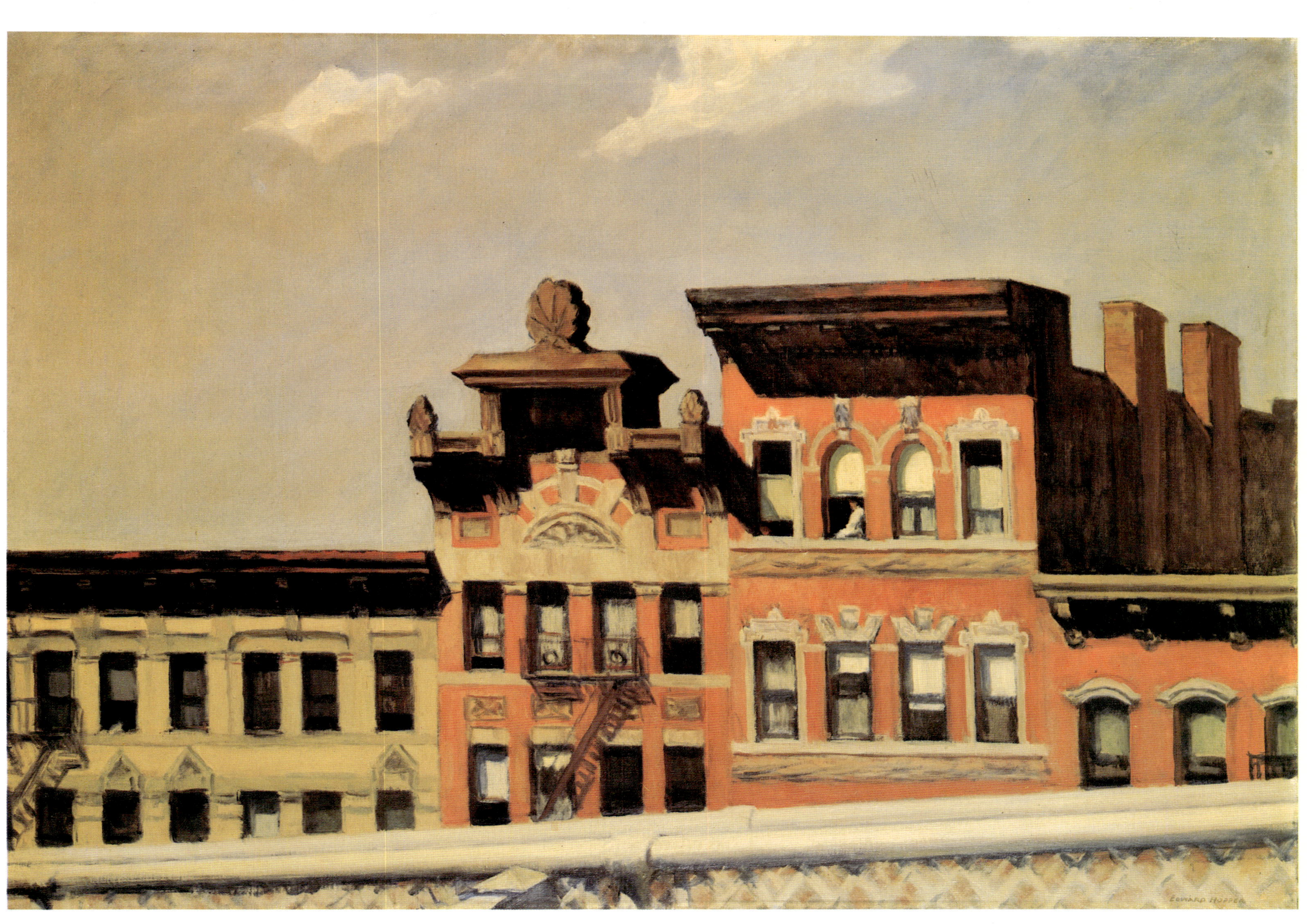

Marsden Hartley, 1877–1943, *American*

LOBSTER FISHERMEN, MAINE (1940–1941)

Hartley, a native of Maine, studied painting in New York and then went in 1912 to Europe. Instead of drifting to Paris like most Americans, he felt drawn to the German Expressionists in Berlin, where he stayed into the early years of the First World War. On returning to New York, he was inevitably attracted to Albert Ryder, who had discovered his own kind of Expressionism. Harley called Ryder his "moonlightist . . . suffering from the weight of the majesty of dream." Hartley then painted in the Southwest, in Nova Scotia, and in Bermuda. In his later years he returned home to Maine, where his boyhood memories sent fresh sparks of poetry through the work based on German Expressionism and Ryder. He knew that he was breathing new strength from his native air, for he said, "The quality of nativeness is colored by heritage, birth, and environment, and it is for this reason that I wish to declare myself a painter from Maine."

Oil on presswood 29¾ × 40⅞"
Hearn Fund, 1942

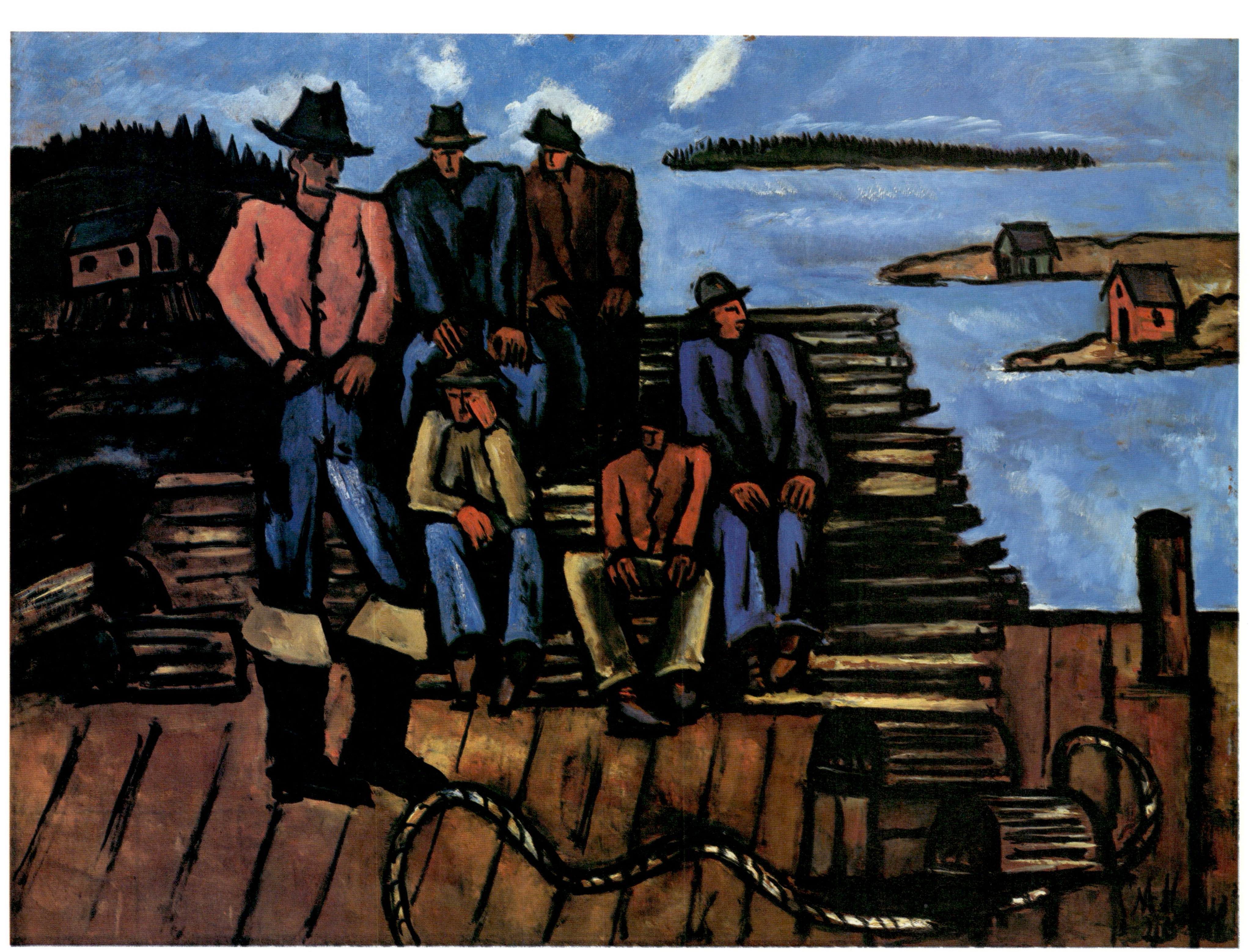

Jack Levine, born 1915, *American*

THE MEDICINE SHOW (1955–1956)

AS A BOY IN BOSTON, Jack Levine studied classical drawing under Denman Ross, whose pupils also tried their hand at various historical painting techniques. Thus he was not afraid to pit himself against the old masters in the rich sensuousness of manipulating oil paint. From Boston he moved to New York in the early heyday of abstract expressionism. But Levine, city born and city bred, has found his world in the thick, throbbing, corruptible humanity of cities. Although his themes are greed, cheating, and injustice, he is too human to pare people down to mere caricature and cannot resist a sneaking affection for his crooks and bullies. Again like Hogarth, Levine does not copy the facts of city life, but dramatizes them in allegory. He said of the *Medicine Show,* "This tableau, while (I hope) plausible, is not based on any situation seen recently. It is based partly on memory, partly on rule, and somewhat on fantasy."

Oil on canvas 72 × 63"
Gift of Hugo Kastor, 1956

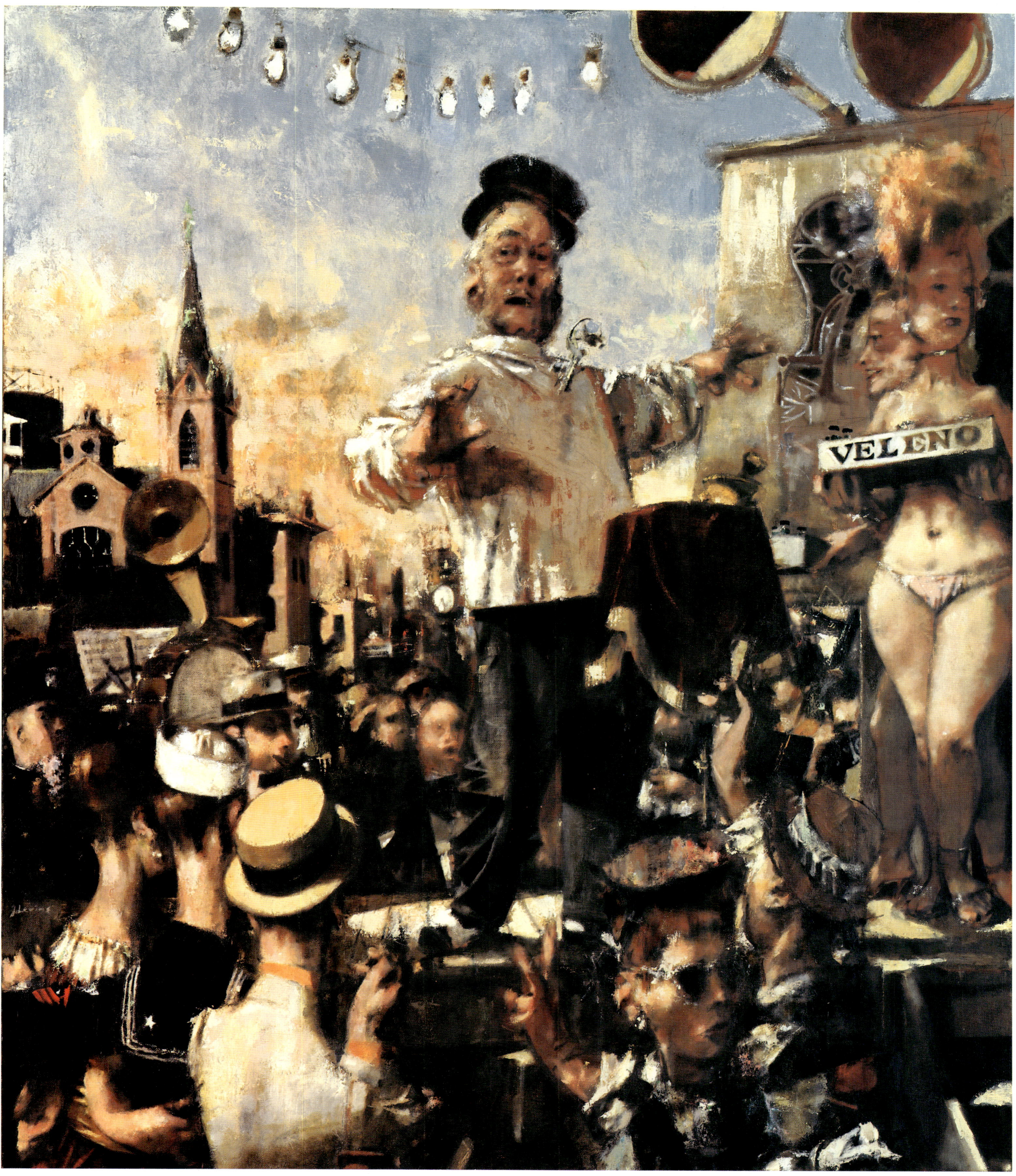
VELENO

ON THE FRONT COVER

Piero del Pollaiuolo, c. 1441, died not later than 1496, *Italian*

PORTRAIT OF A YOUNG WOMAN (detail) (c. 1475)

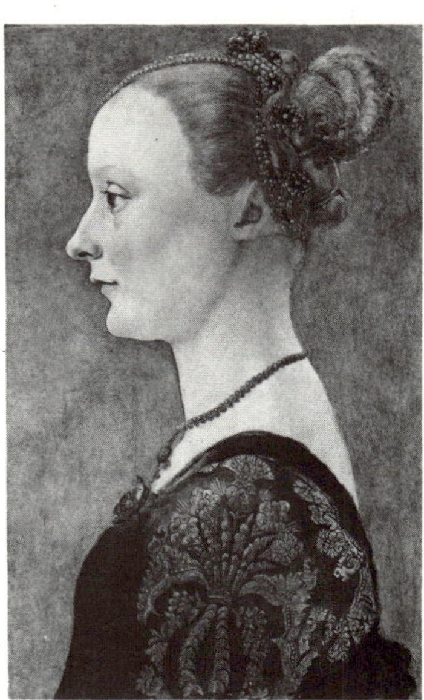

PIERO DEL POLLAIUOLO
Portrait of a Young Woman
Full painting from which cover detail was taken

PROFILE PORTRAITS APPEAR when a revival of classical art creates an admiration for the heads on Greek and Roman coins. Profiles began in Italy about 1400 and returned to all Europe during the classical revival that started about 1770, producing the ultimate profile in the silhouette. This portrait dates from about 1475 when Florentine art was in a magical balance of tradition and discovery. The elaborate coiffure seems to slide off the back of the lady's head because she has plucked out the hair from her forehead. Such a sensitive undershot profile has become rare in our age of orthodontists.

Tempera on wood 19¼ × 13⅞" Bequest of Edward S. Harkness, 1940

ON THE TITLE PAGE

Paul Cézanne, 1839–1906, *French*

THE CARD PLAYERS (c. 1892)

WHEN CÉZANNE PAINTED nudes from imagination, he was free to agitate them in frantic action, but when he painted from live models during many long poses, he had to coddle his victims with comfortable and supported relaxation. Since card players made a suitable quiet group from modern life, he returned to them five times in 1892 and somewhat later with compositions of two to four figures. The French workmen's blue blouses formed irregular cylinders that contrasted interestingly with the flat wall and the cubical table. The workaday setting was probably suggested by a painting of four card players in the manner of Mathieu Le Nain in the museum at Aix. Cézanne said that he painted from memories of museums, discovering new possibilities in old themes. Only the strong and self-reliant dare measure their accomplishment against the masterpieces of the past.

Oil on canvas 25½ × 32" Bequest of Stephen C. Clark, 1960

ON THE BACK COVER

Georges-Pierre Seurat, 1859–1891, *French*

Study for A SUNDAY AFTERNOON AT THE ISLAND OF LA GRANDE JATTE (c. 1884–5)

THIS IS THE FINAL AND MOST complete of Seurat's many studies for his first ambitious painting, now at the Art Institute of Chicago. It represents clerks and shopkeepers avoiding the heat and dust of Paris among the breezes on the river. The banality of the outing accentuates the erudite obliqueness of the treatment. Seurat dabbed pure colors close together to let distance blend them in the eye, the way Newton blended colors on a spinning disk of paper. Seurat's divisions act like the minute dots of red, blue, and yellow blending in the color reproduction that you are looking at. His figures, arrested in profile or full face, must have appeared to his contemporaries as archaic as Egyptian paintings. In fact, the whole picture opposes the program of the Impressionists as drastically as it does that of the academic Salon painters, for it anticipates the static spacing, the impersonal solid geometry of figures by Léger, Balthus, and sometimes Picasso. Seurat took a risk that is astonishing in an artist twenty-seven years old, who was to die at thirty-one. Few lives so short have changed the world so much.

Oil on canvas 27¾ × 41" Bequest of Sam A. Lewisohn, 1951